EndNote Essentials

A Book That Makes Your Scientific Writing Easier

First Edition

By Bengt M. Edhlund

FORM & KUNSKAP AB
INFORMATIONTECHNOLOGY

FORM & KUNSKAP AB • P.O.BOX 4 • S-645 06 STALLARHOLMEN • SWEDEN
+46 152 201 80 • SALES@FORMKUNSKAP.COM • WWW.FORMKUNSKAP.COM

ISBN 978-1-312-89726-7

FOREWORD

Welcome to EndNote Essentials

EndNote is a reference handling software serving authors and other writers of virtually all sciences. The main purpose is to transfer literature references from external databases to the user so that bibliographic data can be used directly in the word processor when citing references in an orderly structure. The availability and structure of external databases vary between sciences. Each discipline has its own conditions, possibilities and limitations.

This publication is focusing on the reference handling principles which are common to all disciplines and we describe the procedures between EndNote, Word and the integration that Cite While You Write or CWYW is about.

Careful emphasis on these important functions and suggestions of practical basic settings and properties and various tips are significant for this publication. The author has gathered experience through courses, lectures and support services from a large number of universities, schools and from the industry.

While the material is structured as course literature and serves an encyclopedia it will also be a strong resource for those who prefer self-studies.

This book is also available in Swedish under the title *Allt om EndNote Essentials.*

Bengt M. Edhlund

Bengt Edhlund has written several books on software including *NVivo 10 Essentials.* Bengt is Scandinavia's leading trainer of academic software. Earlier a telecoms engineer Bengt has the last decades published several books on PubMed, EndNote, NVivo, and Excel. All of Bengt's books are available in Swedish and English. Bengt has trained researchers and students from many corners of the world like Canada, Sweden, Norway, China, Egypt, Uganda and Vietnam. Bengt's training philosophy is to support students by offering good training literature, personal support, and fast and reliable problem solving via Skype or email.

TABLE OF CONTENTS

1. INTRODUCTION TO REFERENCE HANDLING WITH ENDNOTE

The Structure of EndNote Essentials

We have tried to structure our book in a way that allows you to start at the beginning or skip ahead to a section that is of particular interest to you. The current edition describes EndNote X7 for Windows but is to a large extent applicable to other software versions.

Graphic Conventions

In this book we have applied some simple graphic conventions to improve readability and make the material easier to understand.

Example	Comments
Go to **EndNote 7** | **Citations** | **Insert Citation**	Ribbon menu **EndNote 7** and menu group **Citations** and menu option **Insert Citation**
Go to **References → New Reference**	Main menu and submenus in **Bold**
Choose the **Layout** tab	Alternative tabs in **Bold**
Select **Field Shading:** *Always*	Variable in **Bold**; value in *Italic*
Confirm with **[OK]**	Graphic button uses brackets
Use **[Del]**-key to delete	Keyboard key uses brackets
Type `'Bibliography'` in the text box	`Courier` font for typed text
`..[1-3]` will display	`Courier` font for displayed text
..or key command **[Alt]** + **[1]**	Hold the first key while pressing the second

What is a Reference?

All authors are keen on that their publications are registered in the most established scientific databases. The term reference is defined as information that is published in a scientific journal. In the same way as a library applies a system for organizing and classifying all literature also other information is needed to build a complete catalog. Example of such other information is the author names and affiliation, date of publication, journal name and abstract.

We will use the term *record* as a synonym to *reference*. Record is the general term for the items in a database. Even the term *citation* is often used with similar understanding but focused on how the reference will be used.

2. VERIFYING YOUR INSTALLATION

A normal installation of EndNote, on condition that Word is already installed, creates a new Ribbon in Word: **EndNote X7:**

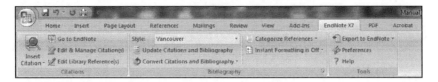

Test from Word that EndNote starts:
- ◆ **Follow These Steps**
  1 Go to **EndNote X7 | Citations | Go to EndNote**
     or [**Alt**] + [**1**].

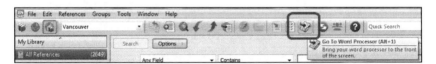

To return to Word:
- ◆ **Follow These Steps**
  1 Go to **Tools → Cite While You Write (CWYW) → Go to Word Processor**
     or [**Alt**] + [**1**]
     or the icon ![icon].

Updates and patches

Software and its applications need to be kept updated continuously and imperfections and improvements are commonplace. This section is about updates and patches that are not new product versions but "fixes" that are possible to download from the supplier.

EndNote has a menu that verifies your current installation having the latest available update (not the latest product version).
- ◆ **Follow These Steps**
  1 Go to **Help → Check for updates...**

You will get a message if you have that latest update or not and if not you can download a patch through your open EndNote directly. Installing this patch you need to have *Administrator's* properties. These updates can also include new configuration files (filters, connection files and styles).

The latest available updates on the day of printing are:

EndNote X5.0.1
EndNote X6.0.1
EndNote X7.2

Software version and updates of your current installation can be verified by going to **Help → About EndNote X7...**

3. IMPORTANT SETTINGS

This section is about user settings in EndNote and Word. The settings are valid individually for each software and the idea behind these suggestions is to make work easier for the user, improve performance and improve communication between EndNote and Word.

EndNote

EndNote's most important settings are located under the title Preferences.

♦   **Follow These Steps**

1   Go to **Edit → Preferences...**

The buttons in the lower row have the following functions:

[**EndNote Defaults**] resets the current panel to EndNote's factory settings.

[**Revert Panel**] resets the current panel to the most recent settings that are saved.

[**OK**] saves settings for the current panel and closes the dialog box.

[**Cancel**] closes the dialog box without saving changed settings.

[**Apply**] saves settings for the current panel without closing the dialog box.

Section Change Case

Contains a list of such words and acronyms that should keep its cases. Type a new word in the upper text box followed by clicking [**Add**]. Words can be deleted by selecting followed by clicking [**Remove**]. Finally save with [**OK**].

Section Display Fields

This is the section where you decide which columns shall be displayed in the open Library window. Maximum 10 columns can be displayed. With the drop-down list below the heading *Field* you can select among the generic field names and below *Heading* you can type your own customized column title. If you do not type any title EndNote will use the generic title. If you want to skip a certain column you select the alternate *[Do not display]*. The checkbox *Display all authors in the Author field* implies that all author's names are shown in one row in this column. See more on this on page 34.

Section Display Fonts

You can choose fonts and size for the text in the Library window, the standard text, the field labels and the search panel.

Section Duplicates

Settings for the conditions for duplicate identification. See more on this on page 39.

Section Find Full Text

This section determines which resources to apply when finding full text items. See more on this on page 66. The option OpenURL is used when your institution has access to an OpenURL server. You add its URL and possible an authentication URL making it necessary to log in to the OpenURL server. The checkbox *Automatically invoke Find Full Text on newly-imported references* implies that after each import of a text file with new references the Find Full Text function is automatically activated.

Section Folder Locations

This section determines the locations for your own edited styles, filters, and connection files. EndNote's default configuration files are located elsewhere.

Section Formatting

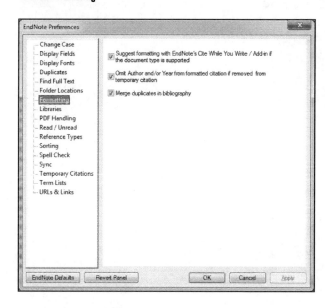

Here are conditions applied during formatting libraries.

Section Libraries

One of the most practical settings is to let EndNote open a certain Library or libraries each time you start EndNote.

♦   **Follow These Steps**
1   Open the Library that you want EndNote to open.
2   Go to **Edit → Preferences** and section *Libraries*.
3   The upper drop-down list: Open the specified libraries.
4   Click **[Add Open Libraries]**.
5   Confirm with **[OK]**.

Section PDF Handling

EndNote can change names of the PDF-files according to the options available here. See more on this on page 74. You can also let EndNote automatically import PDF-files by checking *Enable automatic importing* and defining the folder with [**Select Folder**].

Section Read/Unread

This section makes it possible to mark unread references with bold and specify conditions for when a reference is marked read.

Section Reference Types

More on this on page 32.

Section Sorting

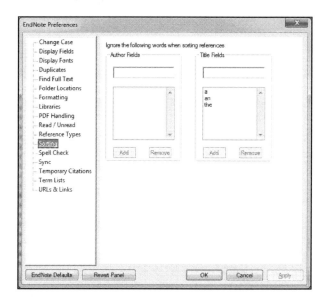

The conditions for sorting are determined here when certain words (often short words) are typed in the upper text box followed by clicking [**Add**]. The result is that these words are ignored when sorting alphabetically the fields Author and Title. See more on this on page 34.

Section Spell Check

Settings for Spell Check. More on this on page 133.

Section Sync

More on this on page 156.

Section Temporary Citations

The temporary citation delimiter, the record number marker and the citation prefix marker are defined here. More on this on pages 77 and 91.

Section Term Lists

We recommend keeping these three checkboxes unchecked. The reasons are explained on page 123.

Section URLs & Links

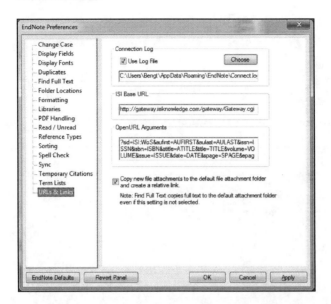

A log file is defined here used when EndNote is connected to external databases.

Word

Certain settings are made in Word Options that you can reach by clicking Word's Office Button in the upper left corner of the window

 and then select Word Options

Click [**Word Options**] and select section *Advanced*:

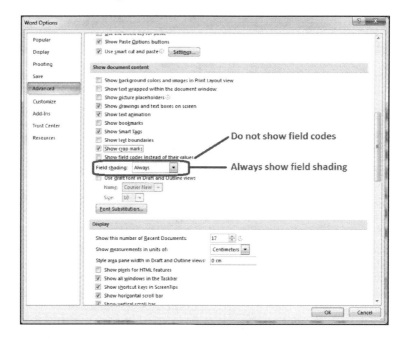

We suggest verifying the following settings:
- Uncheck *Show field codes instead of their values*. The reason is explained later in this book.
- Select Field shading *Always*. This makes viewing and editing citations and bibliographies easier.

Other Settings

Our experience is that the function merely is a source to problems and confusions and sometimes performance disturbances. We suggest that you keep this function inactive. Should you for any reason prefer to use Instant Formatting it is easy to re-activate.

- **Follow These Steps**
  1. Word: Go to **EndNote 7 | Tools | Preferences**
     or key command **[Alt] + [9]**.

  alternatively
  1. EndNote: Go to **Tools → Cite While You Write [CWYW] → Preferences**
     or key command **[Alt] + [9]**.

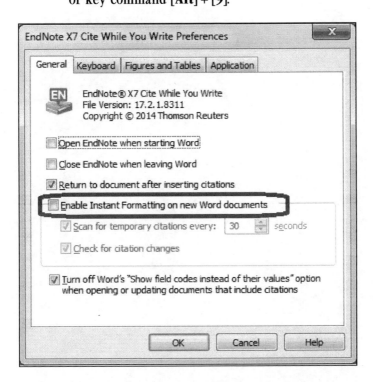

These are our recommended settings and especially the unchecking of *Enable Instant Formatting on new Word documents.*

4. WINDOWS, PANELS AND TOOLBARS IN ENDNOTE

The Library Window

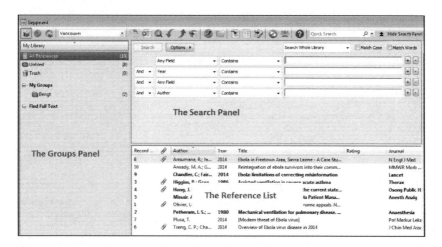

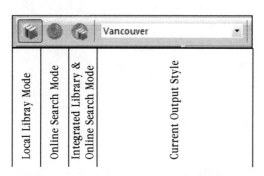

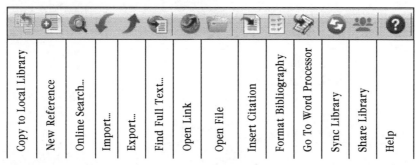

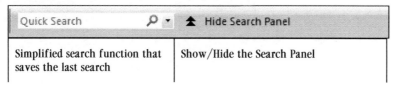

The Tabs Panel or Reference Panel

This panel is placed on the right side of the Library Window and has the tabs Reference (open reference showing all fields), Preview (formatterad reference applying the current style) and PDF (showing the current PDF when it exists).

The **Reference** tab:

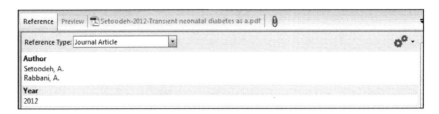

The **Preview** tab:

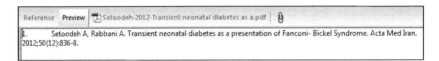

The **Attached PDFs** tab:

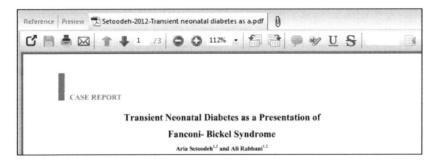

In the Library Window, bottom right, is the layout Control of the Groups Panel and the Reference Panel:

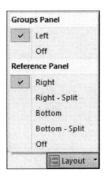

The Reference Window

You need to open a reference in a separate window to get access to all functions and tools.

♦ **Follow These Steps**

    1   Go to **References → Edit References**
        or key command **[Ctrl] + [E]**
        or double click on the reference in the Library.

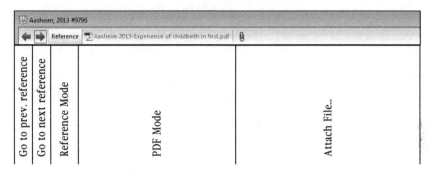

The **Reference** tab:

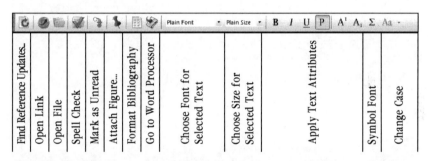

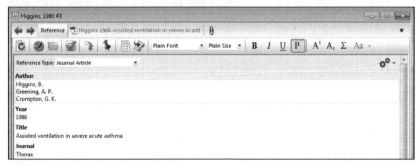

This tab is also available in the Tabs Panel but then the toolbar is not available.

The **Attached PDFs** tab:

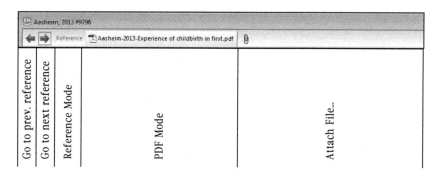

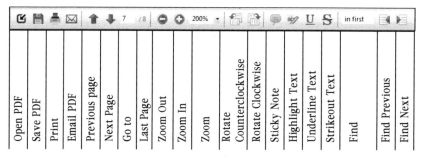

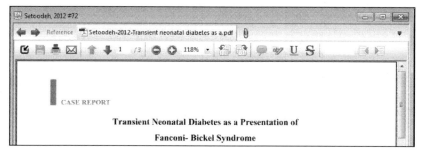

PDFs in the Tabs Panel can reach all functions and tools, but to get a better use of the screen we suggest you open PDFs in a separate window (the Reference Window)

using the icon ⬚. You close again with ⬚.

In the Reference Window, bottom right, is the layout Control of the PDF Panel:

5. HANDLING A LIBRARY

The EndNote Library is a database with a number of records. Each record represents a source of some kind normally a book, a book chapter, a journal article, a legal case, a patent or in principle any kind of literature that a writer needs to cite or refer to.

Each record is built up of a number of fields and each field is dedicated a certain task or certain data organized in a way that it serves different purposes. Spelling is important as any typing error (minor or major) may cause a record not to be found when needed.

An EndNote Library is a file with the file extension *.ENL for EndNote Library. In case of attached data as for example attached files, see further pages 65 and 71.

Creating a New Library

♦   **Follow These Steps**
   1   Go to **File → New...**
   2   Determine a file location and a file name of your Library.
   3   Confirm with **[Save]**.

Where do you store your EndNote Libraries? A Library is at least as precious as a manuscript under production and need to be saved with great care. In most cases it is wise to save a Library in the same folder as your manuscripts and with same backup routines.

Creating New Records

♦   **Follow These Steps**
   1   Create a new record with **References → New Reference**
       or key command **[Alt] + [N]**

       or the icon
       or right-click and select **New Reference**.
   2   Decide applicable Reference Type from the drop-down list.
   3   Type data in respectable fields.
   4   Save with **File → Save** or close the window and approve the question 'Save?'.

You may use **Edit → Undo** or **[Ctrl] + [Z]**, to rest to earlier saved text in any field. When a record is saved and closed the Undo function is not working.

About Reference Types

EndNote X7 has maximum 53 different Reference Types and each of them can consist of maximum 51 fields. The factory default for EndNote X7 defines a preset of Reference Types and fields which can be customized by the user.

♦ **Follow These Steps**

1   Go to **Edit → Preferences**.
2   Select section **Reference Types**.
3   Click **[Modify Reference Types]** and this dialog box is shown:

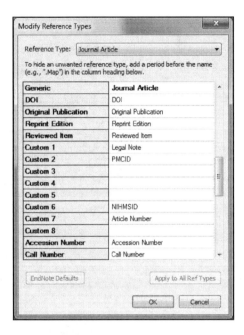

The Reference Type Generic uses all 51 fields with its generic field names, but all other Reference Types can be modified. When you delete a field name then this field will not be used. You can also delete a Reference Type by typing a 'dot' as a prefix to the Reference Type:

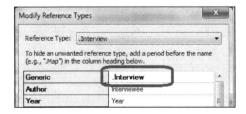

4   Save the settings with **[OK]**.

The customized settings for Reference Types and field names can be exported as a so called XML-file. Such file can then be imported by other users so that same settings can be applied to several users. Factory default is recovered by clicking [**EndNote Defaults**].

About Record Numbers

EndNote assigns each new record a Record Number starting with [#]1. Record Numbers can not be changed by the user. A Record Number of a deleted record can not be used again. Record Numbers are used in the Word manuscript as the internal address from a citation to a record in a certain Library. Each Library has its own numbering series.

About Author Names and Other Personal Names

The following generic fields are used for personal names: Author, Secondary Author, Tertiary Author and Subsidiary Author. Names in these fields must follow certain rules (syntax). The basic rule is that each name needs to be types on a separate row. The following variants are possible:

```
Pettersson, T.G.
Pettersson, TG
Tage G. Pettersson
Tage G Pettersson
Tage Pettersson
van Beethoven, Ludwig
von Euler, F
de la Gardie, Magnus
```

When a name prefix is used like for `von Euler,` the rule is: *Second name, First name.*

The comma is important. If the comma is omitted EndNote will always interpret the last name in the string as Second name.

Viewing and Sorting Libraries

An open Library with all panels can look like this:

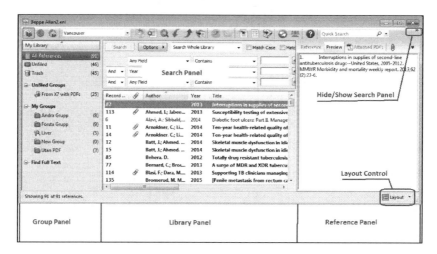

The Layout Control can open and close the Group Panel and the Reference Panel. The latter can also be moved to the right or below the Library Panel or be split in two panels. There is also a button above right that can open or close the Search Panel.

Each record is a row in the Library Panel. The displayed fields (max 10 columns) are determined by the following settings in EndNote.

◆ **Follow These Steps**
1 Go to **Edit → Preferences**.
2 Select the section **Display Fields** and the following dialog box is shown:

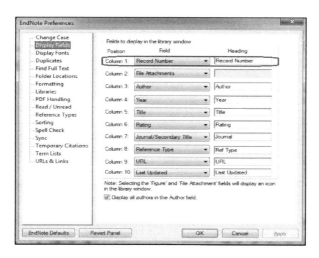

Many users prefer to display the frecords numbers in the Library Panel. The drop-down list for **Column 1** can be used for this purpose. The result of such modification after confirming with [**OK**] is:

Record...	🖉	Author	Year	Title	Rating	Journal	Ref Type
87			2013	Interruptions in supplies of second-line antitub...		MMWR Morb ...	Journal Article
113	🖉	Ahmed, I.; Jabee...	2013	Susceptibility testing of extensively drug-resis...		Antimicrob Ag...	Journal Article
6		Alavi, A.; Sibbald,...	2014	Diabetic foot ulcers: Part II. Management		J Am Acad Der...	Journal Article
11	🖉	Arnoldner, C.; Li...	2014	Ten-year health-related quality of life in cochl...		Laryngoscope	Journal Article
14	🖉	Arnoldner, C.; Li...	2014	Ten-year health-related quality of life in cochl...		Laryngoscope	Journal Article
12		Batt, J.; Ahmed, ...	2014	Skeletal muscle dysfunction in idiopathic pulm...		Am J Respir Cel...	Journal Article
15		Batt, J.; Ahmed, ...	2014	Skeletal muscle dysfunction in idiopathic pulm...		Am J Respir Cel...	Journal Article
85		Behera, D.	2012	Totally drug resistant tuberculosis--a fact or m...		Indian J Tuberc	Journal Article
77		Bernard, C.; Bros...	2013	A surge of MDR and XDR tuberculosis in Franc...		Euro Surveill	Journal Article
114	🖉	Blasi, F.; Dara, M...	2013	Supporting TB clinicians managing difficult cas...		Eur Respir J	Journal Article
135		Bronserud, M. M...	2015	[Penile metastasis from rectum cancer primari...		Ugeskr Laeger	Journal Article
63		Buchanan, L. S.	2014	Do you know what your endodontic instrumen...		Dent Today	Journal Article

A Library can be sorted according to alternatives decided by **Tools → Sort Library...** It is also practical and fast to click the column head in a certain column of the Library Panel. Clicking the column head **Record Number** will display the following sorting:

Record...	🖉	Author	Year	Title	Rating	Journal	Ref Type
5		Gottlieb, B. H.; ...	2014	Social support and adjustment among wives of...		J Psychosoc On...	Journal Article
6		Alavi, A.; Sibbald,...	2014	Diabetic foot ulcers: Part II. Management		J Am Acad Der...	Journal Article
7		Cavalheri, V.; Ta...	2014	Exercise training for people following lung res...		Cancer Treat R...	Journal Article
8		Thomson, L.; Fay...	2014	Life quality and health in adolescents and emer...		Dev Med Child ...	Journal Article
9		Klaassen, R. J.; B...	2014	Validation and reliability of a disease-specific q...		Br J Haematol	Journal Article
10		Ringash, J.; Au, H...	2014	Quality of life in patients with K-RAS wild-type...		Cancer	Journal Article
11	🖉	Arnoldner, C.; Li...	2014	Ten-year health-related quality of life in cochl...		Laryngoscope	Journal Article
12		Batt, J.; Ahmed, ...	2014	Skeletal muscle dysfunction in idiopathic pulm...		Am J Respir Cel...	Journal Article
13		Sandborn, W. J.; ...	2014	Subcutaneous golimumab induces clinical resp...		Gastroenterolo...	Journal Article
14	🖉	Arnoldner, C.; Li...	2014	Ten-year health-related quality of life in cochl...		Laryngoscope	Journal Article
15		Batt, J.; Ahmed, ...	2014	Skeletal muscle dysfunction in idiopathic pulm...		Am J Respir Cel...	Journal Article
16		Cavalheri, V.; Ta...	2014	Exercise training for people following lung res...		Cancer Treat R...	Journal Article
17		Gottlieb, B. H.; ...	2014	Social support and adjustment among wives of...		J Psychosoc On...	Journal Article

A second click on the same column head displays the reversed sorting. The sorting principles can be modified so that some common name prefixes like van, von, de la or other short words like a, an, the are ignored when sorted. Such modifications are made with **Edit → Preferences → Sorting**.

Copying, Cutting and Pasting References

You can organize you Library in many ways. Quite a few users organize one large Master Library while others prefer a number of smaller Libraries. Whichever principle you decide to apply there is often a need of moving or copying records from one Library to another. Some users have a temporary Library for browsing and selecting references before they finally decide to move them to the Master Library.

Selecting Records

Select *one* record using the mouse pointer and *one* click. Several records are selected by pressing the [**Ctrl**]-key and *one* click on the records you want to select. A continuous interval of records are selected by pressing the [**Shift**]-key and clicking the first and last records in the interval. All shown records can be selected with **Edit → Select All** or key command [**Ctrl**] + [**A**].

Cutting Records

♦ **Follow These Steps**

1 Make the 'from' Library active.
2 Select one or more records.
3 Go to **Edit → Cut**
or key command [**Ctrl**] + [**X**]
or right-click and select **Cut**.

Copying Records

♦ **Follow These Steps**

1 Make the 'from' Library active.
2 Select one or more records.
3 Go to **Edit → Copy**
or key command **Ctrl**] + [**C**]
or right-click and select **Copy**.

Pasting Records

♦ **Follow These Steps**

1 Make the 'to' Library active.
2 Go to **Edit → Paste**
or key command [**Ctrl**] + [**V**]
or right-click and select **Paste**.

Drag-and-drop is also possible between Libraries and this method means copying and pasting.

Pasting a record means that an exact copy with all its fields and attachments are inserted in the new Library. Newly pasted records are shown as selected. It is important to know that newly pasted records will have new Record Numbers as every Library has its own record numbering.

Copying a Library

Neither a Library nor a single record has access to the command Save or Save As. These commands are instead available for other functions in EndNote like editing of Filters, Connection files or Styles.

A Library is saved when all records are saved which is when all new and all edited records are closed. In this situation EndNote has instead a special saving command called Save a Copy.

♦   **Follow These Steps**
  1   Go to **File → Save a Copy...**
  2   Select location and file name.

The Library copy that you create is an exact copy using the same record numbering but without groups, attachment folders and attachments. See also more on this on pages 71 and 163 and how to save a compressed Library.

Merging Libraries

Two merging principles exist.

For relatively small Libraries we recommend:

♦   **Follow These Steps**
  1   Make the 'from' Library active.
  2   Select all records with **Edit → Select All**
      or key command **Ctrl] + [A]**.
  3   Go to **Edit → Copy**
      or key command **[Ctrl] + [C]**
      or right-click and select **Copy**.
  4   Make the 'to' Library active.
  5   Go to **Edit → Paste**
      or key command **[Ctrl] + [V]**
      or right-click and select **Paste**.

For relatively large Libraries we recommend:

♦   **Follow These Steps**
  1   Close the 'from' Library.
  2   Make the 'to' Library active.
  3   Go to **File → Import...**

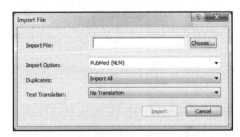

  4   Use [**Choose...**] to find the 'from' Library. Then select
      EndNote Library at the **Import Option** drop-down list.

5 Import with [**Import**].
6 Show all records in the merged Library using **References** →
Show All References
or key command [**Ctrl**] + [**M**]
or right-click and select **Show All References**.

Searching References

◆ **Follow These Steps**
1 Make the Library active.
2 Go directly to the Search Panel if available
or key command [**Ctrl**] + [**F**].

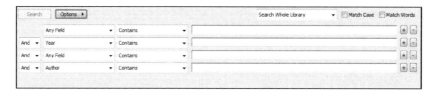

3 Type a search word and select a field with the drop-down
list. The operators And, Or or Not are selected using their
drop-down lists.

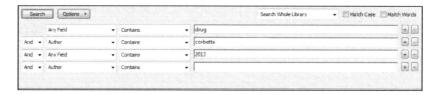

4 Search with [**Search**].
All found records are shown and all other records are temporarily
hidden:

When you want to show all records go to **References – Show All References** or key command **[Ctrl]** + **[M]** or right-click and select **Show All References**.

Various settings of the Search Panel are available when clicking the **[Options]**-button:

Save Search: saving a search expression.

Load Search: using a saved search expression.

Set Default: saves panel size, number of text boxes, selected fields and operators.

Restore Default: revokes the saved settings of the Search Panel but with *blank text boxes.*

Convert to Smart Group: creates a new Smart Group using the current search.

Insert tab: inserts a tab at the cursor.

Insert Carriage Return: inserts a new line at the cursor.

Deleting Records

♦ **Follow These Steps**

1 Select the record or records you want to delete.

2 Go to **Edit → Clear**
or key command **[Ctrl]** + **[D]**.

3 Confirm with **[Yes]**.

Finding Duplicates

The conditions for finding duplicates are set under
Edit → Preferences → Duplicates.

♦ **Follow These Steps**

1 Make the current Library active.

2 Go to **References → Find Duplicates**.

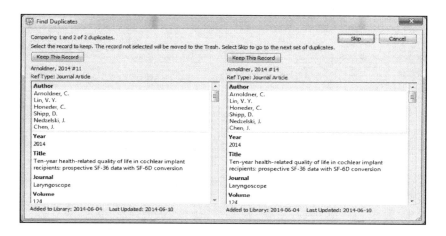

Now you can select which records you want to save and after clicking [**Cancel**] the following list of records is shown:

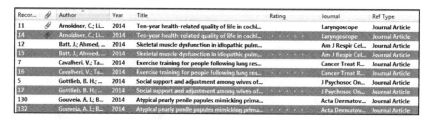

Duplicates found are shown so that all records except the record with the lowest record numbers are selected. Selected records may easily be deleted. Deleted record numbers can not be restored.

Opening a Record and Browsing a Library

♦   **Follow These Steps**

1   Make the current Library active.

2   Select *one* record and go to
References → Edit References
or key command [**Qtrl**] + [**E**]
or right-click and select **Edit References**
or [**Enter**]
or double-click on the selected record.

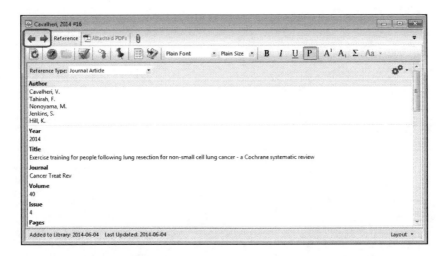

3 Browse through the records in the current sort order with the Next/Previous-buttons in the upper left corner of the reference window

or **References → Next Reference**

or **[Ctrl] + [PgDn]**.

alternatively

4 Go to **References → Previous Reference**

or **[Ctrl] + [PgUp]**.

Please note, that when a certain field has been chosen with a pointer click a frame is shown surrounding the chosen field. This is normal edit mode for a field. First time record is opened the Author field is in edit mode. However, any field may be selected in a record and when browsing the same field is shown in edit mode for all records.

6. TRANSFER REFERENCES FROM SCIENTIFIC DATABASES

Three different methods of transferring data (references) from scientific databases to EndNote are prevailing. Which method you prefer is a personal matter and also depending on properties and functionalities offered by the database provider.

The three methods are:

- Online searching from EndNote
- Import of a text file using a filter
- Direct Export from external database to EndNote

Online Search in a new way

When the new Group Panel was introduced EndNote has a new way to use and connect its favorite Connection Files.

The first time a Connection File is used, for example PubMed (NLM), you go to **Tools → Online Search...** and the whole list of Connection Files is shown. You select a Connection File and click the **[Choose]**-button. Then a new group is created under the heading Online Search. The group is called PubMed (NLM) and you are logged in and the Search Panel is connected to the external source.

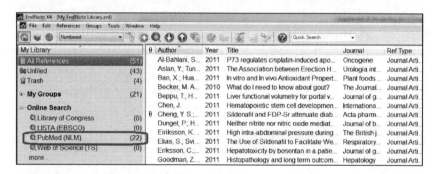

When a search and retrieval has been completed the number of retrieved records is shown within parenthesis. Next connection and search can easily be made by clicking the name PubMed (NLM).

Three Operating Modes

EndNote has the following three operating modes that are available with buttons on the left side of the toolbar of the Library window:

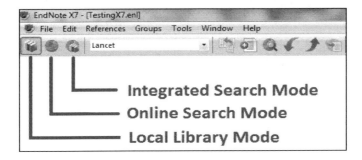

- ◆ *Local Library Mode* means that you only work within your own Library.

- ◆ *Online Search Mode* means that the result of online searching is stored in a temporary Library and thereafter you need to select which records you want to copy to your Library. A method recognized by previous EndNote users.

- ◆ *Integrated Search Mode* means that the result f online searching is stored directly in your current Library. There is an obvious risk that you will get obsolete or redundant records in your Library!

The operation mode that prevails when you close a Library is current next time you open that Library.

Online Searching with EndNote

Choose *Online Search Mode.* Avoid Integrated Search Mode as the result of your searches is directly added to your Library without you having full control.

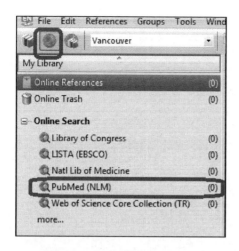

PubMed (NLM) is by default marked as a favorite and is a Connection File that includes a filter function. After clicking you are logged in on PubMed on condition you are connected to the Internet.

The Search Panel looks like this:

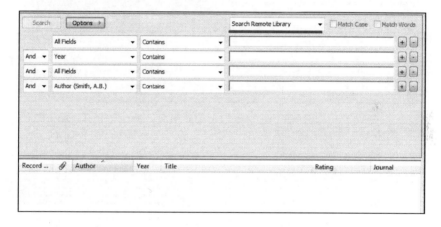

The verification that you are connected to PubMed is that the text box Search Remote Library is active.

You can now fill in the search form based on your knowledge and experience of PubMed, like for example:

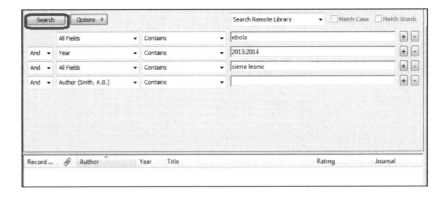

Now you click the [**Search**]-button and the response may be:

If you accept to capture these 78 records you click [**OK**]. When all records are captured it looks like this:

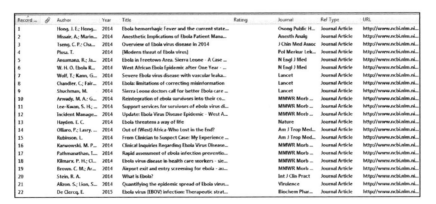

The sort order is now determined by PubMed which is the most recent on top and then descending. Next step is to transfer selected records to your Library. Select all or select only the records you want to transfer.

Right-click and select **Copy References To** and go to the current Library **Beppe.enl**. Alternatively, go to **References → Copy References To → Beppe.enl**

Finally, go to your current Library with Local Library Mode and it may look like this:

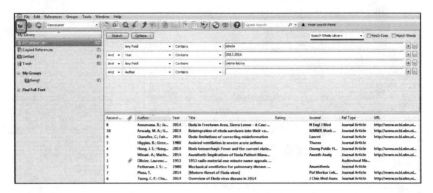

In this case we had 3 records from before and now we have added 7 new. All records have Record Numbers and the sorting is by default alphabetic (first Author) but can be changed by clicking any column head.

When you want to open and study a reference you double-click and it is displayed like this:

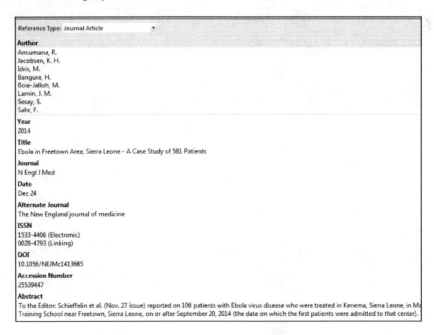

The Connection Manager

A large number of Connection Files are delivered with EndNote. Tools for editing and creating new Connections are included. When editing a standard Connection File you normally keep the original file intact and instead create a copy. Modification and editing is made in EndNote's Connection Manager.

♦ **Follow These Steps**

1 Go to **Edit → Connection Files → Open Connection Manager...**

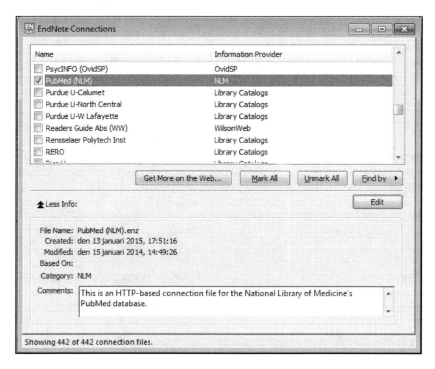

2 Select a Connection File for example *PubMed (NLM)*.

3 Click [**Edit**].

We will explain some of the settings that in a Connection File. You can make modficatons and the save with **File → Save** or [**Ctrl**] + [**S**] and EndNote will suggest to create a copy that is stored in the folder defined on page 17.

Section **Connection Settings** stores the external server address and other basic settings making it possible to log in to external databases and libraries:

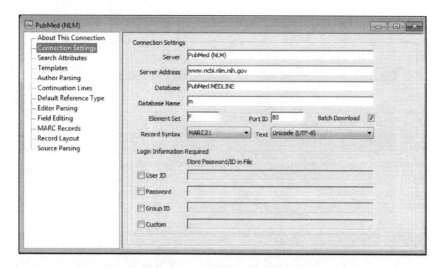

Section **Search Attributes** defines the fields available in the Search Panel after connecting to the database:

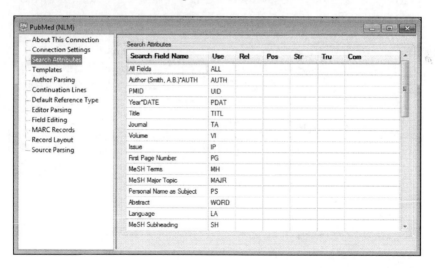

Section **Templates** is a filter function that translates the external databases' format to the native fields and reference types of EndNote:

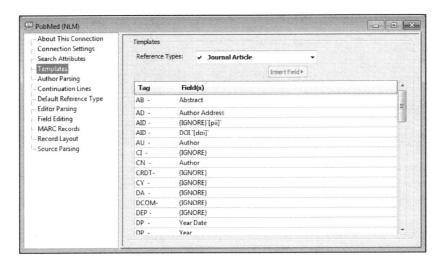

The connection Status

During the ongoing work session you can follow the communication between EndNote and the external database.

♦ **Follow These Steps**

1 Go to **Windows → Show Connection Status**

The *Status Messages* option displays EndNote's search string created from the Search Panel. The *Record Data* option displays the response as data string with new references.

Import of a Text File Using a Filter

This is the oldest method to capture references from an external database. You let the database create and download a tagged text file with data from the selected references. This text file is then imported using an import filter unique to each database provider and database. The filter is then translating the externa database format to EndNote's referene types and fields.

PubMed can create a text file that easily can be imported to a reference handling software like EndNote. We summarize the procedure in PubMed:

• Mark the references that you want to download. No marking means all shown references.
• Go to **Send to** and select *File*.
• Choose the format *MEDLINE* from the drop-down list.
• Click [**Create File**].

- Finally you need to decide location and file name. PubMed will suggest the file name 'pubmed_result.txt' but this name can be changed. This text file must then be imported using an import filter that translates PubMed's MEDLINE-format to the native format of the used reference handling software.

♦ **Follow These Steps**

1 Open the EndNote Library where the references will reside.

2 Go to **File → Import → File...**

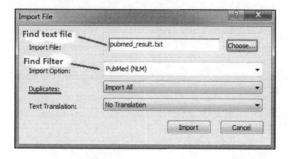

3 Use **[Choose]** to find the text file.

4 With **Import Option** drop-down list you will find the proper filter for your text file.

5 You can prevent duplicates from being imported by selecting *Discard Duplicates* at the **Duplicates** drop-down list.

6 Click **[Import]**.

The Filter Manager

A large number of Import Filters are delivered with EndNote. Tools for editing and creating new Filters are included. When editing a standard Filter you normally keep the original file intact and instead create a copy. Modification and editing is made in EndNote's Filter Manager.

♦ **Follow These Steps**

1   Go to **Edit → Import Filters → Open Filter Manager...**

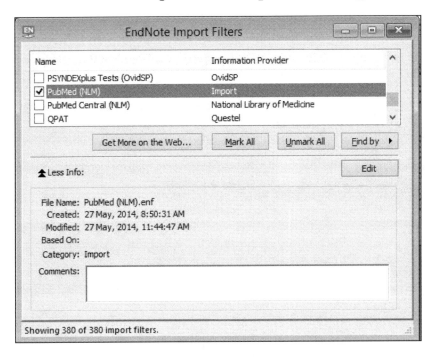

2   Select a Filter, for example *PubMed (NLM)*.

3   Click [**Edit**].

We will explain some of the settings that in a Filter. You can make modfications and the save with **File → Save** or [**Ctrl**] + [**S**] and EndNote will suggest creating a copy that is stored in the folder defined on page 17.

Section **Templates** is the filter functions that translate the tags of the external database to EndNote's native reference types and fields:

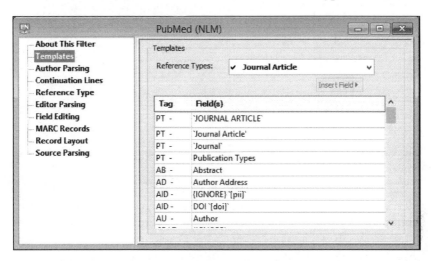

Direct Export from External Database

This method has been used for some time now and was first developed by some commercial database providers. The basic principle is that the external database creates a text file with such properties and a file extension that the reference handling software automatically starts in an import mode and selects the proper import filter.

This lead to a large number of variants as the number of database providers and the number of databases is large and the number of reference handling software has also increased.

The ambition to reach a de facto standard has resulted in PubMed having a standardized format for Direct Export that the developers of reference handling software must adopt to.

The Direct Export function in PubMed is called **Send to → Citation manager** while in other databases this feature is often called Export to EndNote.

The procedure is very much simplified:

- Mark the citations that you want to capture. No markings means all shown citations.
- Go to **Send to** and select *Citation manager*.
- Decide the number of records that you want to transfer and from what starting number. Maximum 200 records can be transferred at a time.
- Click [**Create File**].

Provided your reference handling software is compatible with PubMed's requirements for Direct Export the records will be automatically transferred and stored automatically.

EndNote will be activated and if EndNote is not open it will open and the records will be automatically imported to the default Library using an automatically chosen filter.

If a default Library has not been selected you will be asked to select a Library for this import.

If EndNote is open the uppermost Library will be activated for import from the Direct Export.

7. ABOUT GROUPS

Every Library in EndNote X7 can create groups or subsets of selected references in the following manner:

General Groups

- ◆ *All References* (default group)
- ◆ *Unfiled* (references not belonging to any group)
- ◆ *Trash* (references that have been deleted during ongoing session)
- ◆ *Imported References* (*) (references that have been imported using a filter)
- ◆ *Online Search* (*) (references that have been captured by searching with EndNote)
- ◆ *Search Results* (*) (is created upon each search within the Library)
- ◆ *EndNote Web* (references downloaded from EndNote Online)
- ◆ *Find Full Text* (*) (references that have URLs or PDFs)

Groups marked with (*) are temporary groups existing only during ongoing session and as long as the Library is open.

Custom Groups

The user can create maximum 500 groups in each Library. A reference can belong to more that one group but a reference can only exist once in each group.

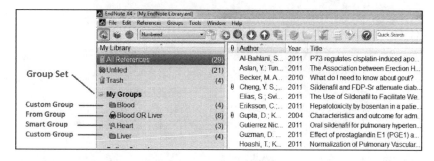

The Group Panel is placed to the left of the Library Window. You can hide and show the Group Panel as follows:

- ◆ **Follow These Steps**
  1   Go to **Groups → Hide Groups/Show Groups**.

Creating a new Group

♦ **Follow These Steps**
  1. Go to **Groups → Create Group**
     or right-click in the Group Panel and select **Create Group**.
  2. Replace the name *New Group* with your own choice of a meaningful name.

Deleting a Group

♦ **Follow These Steps**
  1. Mark the name of the group you want to delete.
  2. Go to **Groups → Delete Group**
     or right-click and select Delete Group.
  3. Confirm with [**Delete**] in the dialog box. Check *Do not show this message again* if you wish to avoid this message in the future.

Adding References to a Group

♦ **Follow These Steps**
  1. Select the reference or references that you want go add to a group.
  2. Go to **Groups → Add References To** and point at the group you want to add references to
     or right-click and select **Add References To**.

Deleting References from the Group

♦ **Follow These Steps**
  1. Mark the group you want to delete a reference or references from.
  2. Select the reference or references that you want to delete from he group.
  3. Go to **Groups → Remove References From Group**.
  4. Confirm with [**Delete**] in the dialog box. Check *Do not show this message again* if you wish to avoid this message in the future.

A practical comment: Working with CWYW and the function *Find Citation* (when you want to choose references without leaving Word) will not let you benefit from groups for large Libraries. Then it is easier to go to EndNote, select the group, select the reference and use the command *Insert Citation(s)*.

Smart Groups

Using Smart Groups is based on a search criterion in your Library that automatically adds new references to a Smart Group. All Smart Groups are listed in the Group Panel and with a click you display its references.

♦   **Follow These Steps**
   1   Go to **Groups → Create Smart Group** and this dialog box is shown:

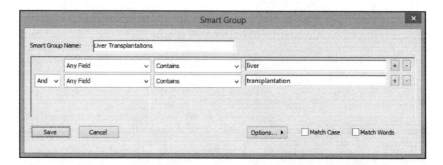

Type the name of the Smart Group and add the search criterion for example:
"Any Field Contains *liver*" AND "Any Field Contains *transplantation*".
   2   Click [**Save**].

Changing name of the group and modifications of the search criterion is made by marking the group name in the Group Panel, right-clicking and selecting **Rename Group** respectively **Edit Group...** Deleting a group is made with right-clicking and selecting **Delete Group**.

Group Sets and From Groups

New features were introduced in EndNote X3 och X4: *Group Sets* and *From Groups*.

Group Sets

A Group Set is a heading for a number of Custom or Smart Groups designed so that the heading represents the logic sum (operator OR) of the underlaying groups. There is alwas at least one Group Set in EndNote that by default is called My Groups. Each Custom Group or Smart Group must belong to a Group Set.

♦   **Follow These Steps**
   1   Go to **Groups → Create Group Set**

The result is a group set called **New Group Set** which needs to be renamed by right-clicking and selecting **Rename Group Set**.

When new groups are created they will be placed under one of the available Group Sets. When you make a selection of new references you may either go to **Groups → Create Group** and a new group will be added under the first (uppermost) Group Set of the Group Panel.

You can also go to **Groups → Add References To** and then select the Group Set and the Group that your references will be added to or right-click and select **Add References To**.

From Groups

You may also create a group that is a logic expression (And, Or or Not) of several other groups.

♦ **Follow These Steps**

    1   Go to **Groups → Create From Groups...**

The dialog box **Create From Groups** is shown:

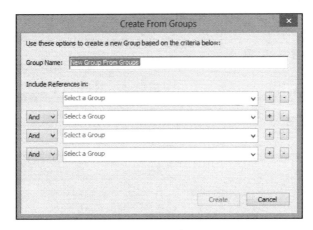

    2   Type the new group name in the **Group Name** text box.

    3   Then select Custom or Smart Group and operator.

    4   Confirm with [**Create**].

8. ENDNOTE CAN BE OPTIMIZED FOR PUBMED

For those who mainly work with references from PubMed there are possibilities to optimize settings in EndNote so that a record in EndNote corresponds to a record in PubMed. This is an example from PubMed in Single Citation View:

Publication Types, MeSH Terms, Substances

Publication Types
Review

MeSH Terms
Antitubercular Agents/adverse effects
Apolipoproteins E/blood
Arylamine N-Acetyltransferase/genetics
Arylamine N-Acetyltransferase/metabolism
Azetidines/adverse effects
Benzylamines/adverse effects
Biological Markers/blood*
Diclofenac/adverse effects
Diclofenac/analogs & derivatives
Drug-Induced Liver Injury/diagnosis*
Drug-Induced Liver Injury/pathology*
Floxacillin/adverse effects
HLA-B Antigens/adverse effects
Humans
Liver/drug effects
Liver/pathology
Metabolomics
Pharmacogenetics
Polymorphism, Genetic
Proteomics
Risk Factors

Substances
Antitubercular Agents
Apolipoproteins E
Azetidines
Benzylamines
Biological Markers
HLA-B Antigens
HLA-B*57:01 antigen
lumiracoxib
Diclofenac
Floxacillin
ximelagatran
Arylamine N-Acetyltransferase
NAT2 protein, human

The fields **Publication Types** and **Substances** do not exist in EndNote's default settings. The MeSH-terms are usually under the field Keywords in EndNote.

It is reasonably easy to make some settings in EndNote to adjust for this. Go to **Edit → Preferences** and the section **Reference Types**.

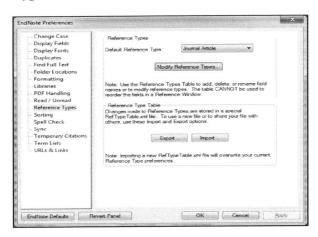

The generic names Custom 3, Custom 4 and Keywords can be changed to Substances, Publication Types and MeSH Terms respectively. These settings can also be exported to other computers using the [**Export...**]-button. The file format of exported settings is XML. The computer that will reproduce these settings will use the [**Import...**]-button.

The button [**Modify Reference Types...**] offers an option to modify the field names. Save with [**OK**].

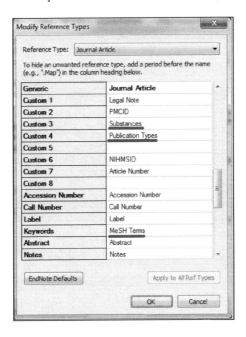

Filter Modification

The next step in optimizing EndNote is to modify a few of the configuration files, the Connection File *PubMed (NLM).enz* and the Filter *PubMed (NLM).enf*. This is necessary for importing data from these fields:

RN - is defined as (Substances)
PT - is defined as Publication Types
PT - is eliminated from the field Notes

To make this work the modified configuration files must be saved with same names and in the same locations as the original files. Normal Windows-conventions must be applied. Normally EndNote will add 'copy' to modified configuration files and save then in a separate folder. After this modification the same reference as above will look like this in EndNote:

Substances
Antitubercular Agents
Apolipoproteins E
Azetidines
Benzylamines
Biological Markers
HLA-B Antigens
HLA-B*57:01 antigen
lumiracoxib
Diclofenac
Floxacillin
ximelagatran
Arylamine N-Acetyltransferase
NAT2 protein, human

Publication Types
Journal Article
Review

MeSH Terms
Antitubercular Agents/adverse effects
Apolipoproteins E/blood
Arylamine N-Acetyltransferase/genetics/metabolism
Azetidines/adverse effects
Benzylamines/adverse effects
Biological Markers/*blood
Diclofenac/adverse effects/analogs & derivatives
Drug-Induced Liver Injury/*diagnosis/*pathology
Floxacillin/adverse effects
HLA-B Antigens/adverse effects
Humans
Liver/drug effects/pathology
Metabolomics
Pharmacogenetics
Polymorphism, Genetic
Proteomics
Risk Factors

Term Lists

You can create Term List from the terms in the Substances AND Publication Types fields. More on Term Lists on page 123.

♦ **Follow These Steps**
1 Go tools **Tools → Define Term Lists...** and then the **Lists** tab and the [**Create List...**]-button.
2 Type *Substances* and then [**OK**].
3 Return to [**Create List...**] and type *Publication Types* and then [**OK**].
4 Finally you need to link certain fields to certain Term Lists by going to [**Link Lists...**]. The settings are:

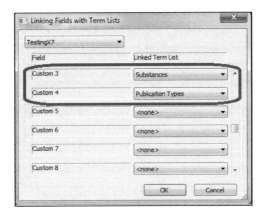

5 Confirm with [**OK**].

Term Lists should be kept updated and always mirror the references in the current Library. One known problem is that when a reference is deleted from a Library the linked terms are not deleted from the Term Lists. Automatic update can also sometimes fail. Therefore we suggest that from time to time zero set an important Term List and then update.

♦ **Follow These Steps**
1 Go to **Tools → Open Term Lists → <name> Term List**.
2 Select all terms with [**Ctrl**] + [**A**].
3 Click [**Delete Term**].
4 Finish with [**Close**].

Then the whole Term List must be manually updated.

♦ **Follow These Steps**
1 Select the references you want to update.
2 Go to **Tools → Define Term Lists...**
3 Select a Term List.
4 Click [**Update List**].
5 Check *Update terms from selected references.*
6 Then [**OK**], finally [**Close**].

When new references are added to the Library linked Term Lists will be automatically updated depending on the settings made under **Edit → Preferences** section **Term Lists,** see page 22 .

A practical use of term lists is when searching references in your own Library.

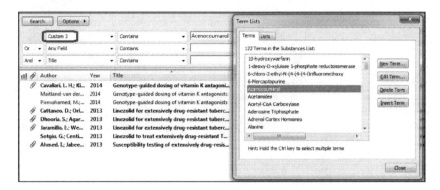

♦ **Follow These Steps**

1   Use Local Library Mode.
2   In the Search Panel select the field corresponding to the linked Term List, for example Custom 3 for Substances.
3   Use key command **[Ctrl]** + **[1]** to open the Term List.
4   Select *one* term.
5   Click **[Insert Term]**, then **[Close]**.
6   Add more terms if you need, then finally **[Search]**.

Updating Your References

Some "preliminary" references are added to PubMed before they are finally indexed with keywords and other terms. The reason is to make important research results available without delay. Such references are assigned 'PubMed in Process' or 'PubMed – as supplied by publisher'.

Eventually these references will be completely indexed with Publication Types, Substances and MeSH Terms why it is a good idea to update such references and the term lists.

Therefore, EndNote has introduced an update function for these preliminary references.

♦ **Follow These Steps**

1   Select the reference or references you want to update.
2   Go to **References → Find Reference Updates...**
3   EndNote displays a picture for each reference that is due for update.
4   If you accept the update then click **[Update all fields->]**
5   Finally click **[Save updates]**.
6   EndNote asks 'Are you sure?'. Confirm with **[Yes]**.

Now you also need to update your term lists as described above.

An Optimal Set of PubMed Configuration Files is:
- PubMed (NLM).enf (Filter)
- PubMed (NLM).enz (Connection File)
- PubMed Optimal.xml (modified fields of Reference Types)

The term lists suggested above need to be created for each new Library.

9. FULL TEXT PDFs AND OTHER FILE ATTACHMENTS

Attached files in EndNote X7 are called **File Attachments**. Such files have relative or absolute locations. EndNote has also the drag-and-drop option to create links to documents and are represented by PDF icons in the File Attachments field. Maximum 45 PDF-links can be created in each reference.

This section is also valid for handling links to other types of files and the type of file is recognized by the icons in the File Attachment field.

Creating Links

♦   **Follow These Steps**

1   Select or open the reference that you want to link from.

2   Go to **References → File Attachments → Attach File...**

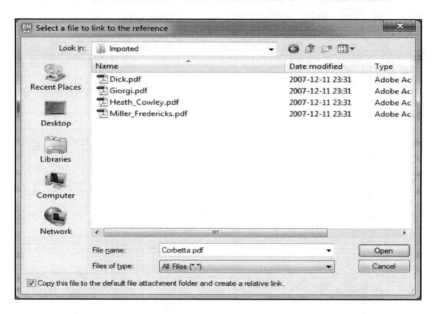

3   Browse to the file you want to link to, select and confirm with **[Open]**.

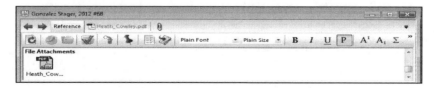

The visible result is a new icon in the File Attachments field. When the *Copy this file to the default file attachment folder and create a relative link* (see above) is checked a relative link has been created. It means that a copy of the PDF-file has been created in the attachment folder of each EndNote Library.

The folder structure is as follows:

If the Library is:

..\My Documents\Bengt.enl and the PDF is CritCare.pdf

Then the copy of the PDF-file is now in this location:

..\My Documents\Bengt.DATA\PDF\0451790553\CritCare.pdf

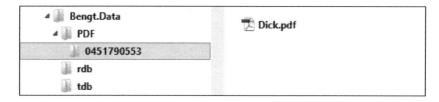

Each file with a relative link is located in a separate folder within Bengt.DATA\PDF\.

If you as an alternative want to create an absolute link to a PDF then uncheck *Copy this file to the default file attachment folder and create a relative link.* The absolute link leads instead to the original file and no relative link will be created.

How can you see the difference between a relative and an absolute link?

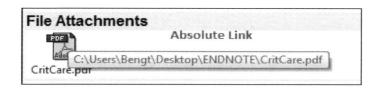

The easiest way is to point at the PDF icon and then the file name only will be shown for a relative link and the complete file path will be shown for an absolute link.

New Function – Find Full Text

EndNote X2 introduced a new way to capture full text articles for primarily such references that are downloaded from PubMed and Web-of-Science. The accessibility is dependent on the user properties. The settings made on page 16 are specifying the resources used for finding full text articles.

♦ **Follow These Steps**

1 Select the reference or references for which you want to find fulltext links.

2 Go to References → Find Full Text

or the icon .

EndNote now searches on the internet for full text articles, usually PDF, and downloads them as relative links attached to respective reference in the EndNote Library.

When a URL requires a password the article is not captured but the URL is then copied to the first position of the URL-field.

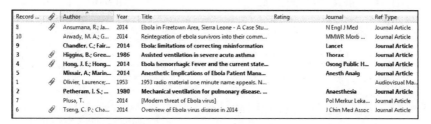

Record ...	🔗	Author	Year	Title	Rating	Journal	Ref Type
8	🔗	Ansumana, R.; Ja...	2014	Ebola in Freetown Area, Sierra Leone - A Case Stu...		N Engl J Med	Journal Article
10		Arwady, M. A.; G...	2014	Reintegration of ebola survivors into their comm...		MMWR Morb ...	Journal Article
9		Chandler, C.; Fair...	2014	Ebola: limitations of correcting misinformation		Lancet	Journal Article
3	🔗	Higgins, B.; Gree...	1986	Assisted ventilation in severe acute asthma		Thorax	Journal Article
4	🔗	Hong, J. E.; Hong...	2014	Ebola hemorrhagic Fever and the current state...		Osong Public H...	Journal Article
5		Missair, A.; Marin...	2014	Anesthetic Implications of Ebola Patient Mana...		Anesth Analg	Journal Article
1	🔗	Olivier, Laurence;...	1953	1953 radio material one minute name appeals. N...			Audiovisual Ma...
2		Petheram, I. S.; ...	1980	Mechanical ventilation for pulmonary disease. ...		Anaesthesia	Journal Article
7		Plusa, T.	2014	[Modern threat of Ebola virus]		Pol Merkur Leka...	Journal Article
6	🔗	Tseng, C. P.; Cha...	2014	Overview of Ebola virus disease in 2014		J Chin Med Assoc	Journal Article

The clip symbols tells you which PDFs are found and captured.

Open and Edit a PDF

There are many ways to open a PDF.

Alternative 1:

♦ **Follow These Steps**

1 Go to **References → File Attachments → Open File**
or [**Ctrl**] + [**Alt**] + [**P**].

This command will open the standard software for the file type in the Attachment field, usually Acrobat Reader. Depending on which software is installed in your computer certain functions are available. If you for example have Acrobat Professional installed then you have more editing functions than for Acrobat Reader. If you edit, save and close such window every modification will be made visible using the next alternative here below.

Alternative 2:

In the Tab Panel click the PDF-tab. Here you can use the most of the editing tools that usually Acrobat Pro offers:

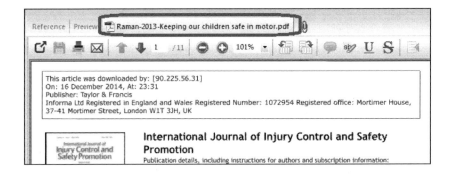

International Journal of Injury Control and Safety Promotion
Publication details, including instructions for authors and subscription information:

If you then click the icon [icon] to the left in the panel the PDF will be shown in a separate undocked window that can be maximized to cover the whole screen, like this:

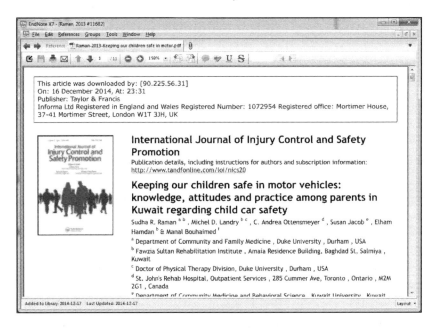

The same toolbar is available in both cases. The most important editing functions are:

- Highlight Text (yellow)
- Sticky Notes
- Underline Text
- Strikeout Text

Furthermore, you can zoom, browse, turn, find text, print and mail.

To close the separate undocked window, use [icon].

Open a Link

You open a link with a click on the icon in the Attachment field or by marking or opening the reference and go to **References → File Attachments → Open File** or using the icon on the toolbar or key command **[Ctrl] + [Alt] + [P]**.

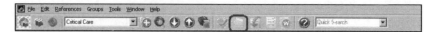

If there are more than one link in the Attachment field EndNote will open the first link.

Deleting a Link

When you delete a relative link the file and its own folder are deleted. Deleting an absolute link removes the link only and the original file is left intact.

♦   **Follow These Steps**
1   Select the icon in the Attachment field.
2   Go to **Edit → Clear**
    or use the **[Del]**-key.

Change an Absolute Link to a Relative Link

It is possible to change absolute links to relative links in a certain reference.

♦   **Follow These Steps**
1   Select or open a certain reference.
2   Go to **References → File Attachments → Convert to Relative Links**.

Preference to Absolute Links

You can set Preferences to Absolute links for all new file attachments, see page 23. Observe, that the function Find Full Text always creates relative links independently from the described settings.

◆ **Follow These Steps**

    1   Go to **Edit → Preferences → URLs & Links**.

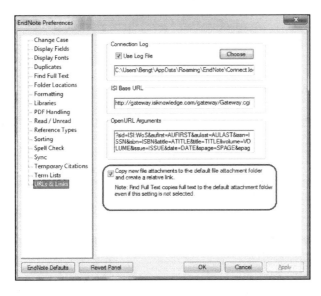

    3   Uncheck Copy new file attachments to the default file attachment folder and create a relative link.

    4   Confirm with [**OK**].

This setting changes the default setting when you create new links and can be changed from situation to situation. The result of using drag-and-drop will be affected by this setting.

Saving and Compressing a Library

EndNote X7 offers a new way to save a Library and its folders and attachments as a zipped file with the file extension *.enlx. The information of Custom Groups and Smart Groups are also stored in the zipped file.

◆ **Follow These Steps**

    1   Open the Library that you want to compress.

    2   Go to **File → Compressed Library (.enlx)**

The following dialog box appears:

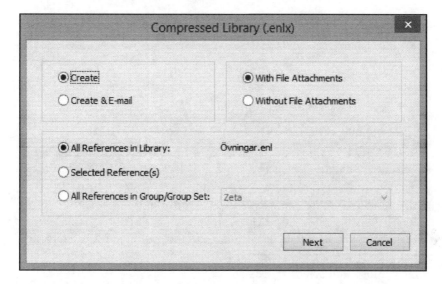

    3   Select the options that this dialog box offers. Click **[Next]**.

    4   Decide file location and file name of the new compressed Library.

    5   Confirm with **[Save]**.

A compressed Library is unpacked with a normal opening command like **File → Open Library...** or key command **[Ctrl]** + **[O]**.

Displaying Links in the Library Window

EndNote X7 can display maximum 10 columns from different fields in the Library window while earlier versions of EndNote could display 5 or 8 columns. The field File Attachments can display a clip symbol when there is any link attached and the field Figures can display a marker when there is an attached figure or graph. See further page 14 about settings of Display Fields.

📊	📎	Author ▲	Year	Title	Journal	Ref Type
✓		Andersson	2006	En annan tabell		Chart or Ta...
		Anwar	1995	The investigation of Epstein-Barr vira...	Cancer	Journal Arti...
		Appelros	2007	A national stroke quality register: 12 ...	European J...	Journal Arti...
	📎	Arslan	2007	Simultaneous hydatid cysts of both th...	Acta Medic...	Journal Arti...
		Arthur	2008	Platelet receptor redox regulation	Platelets	Journal Arti...

File Attachment

Figure

Importing and Creating New References from PDF files

This function was introduced in EndNote X4, and makes it possible to convert a single PDF or a collection of PDFs to EndNote references with a minimum of manual work by letting EndNote extract the DOI-number (Digital Object Identifier) from the PDF files. The procedure is matching the DOI-number with data från CrossRef (www.CrossRef.org) and then transfer bibliographic data to EndNote. This works fine for most journal articles, conference proceedings, dissertations and scientific reports.

In some cases, using EndNote X6 and X7, you can in the next instant use **References → Find Reference Updates...** to get more data on a certain reference.

Importing a single PDF
- ♦ **Follow These Steps**
  1. Open the Library where you want to store the imported PDF-files.
  2. Go to **File → Import → File...**

  The dialog box **Import File** is shown:

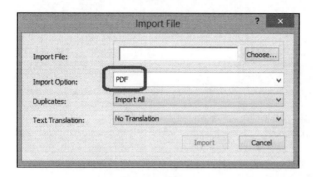

  3. Use [**Choose...**] to find the PDF-file you want to import.
  4. Select Import Option *PDF.*
  5. Select other options.
  6. Import with [**Import**].

Importing a Collection of PDFs
- ♦ **Follow These Steps**
  1. Open the Library where you want to store a collection of PDF-files.
  2. Go to **File → Import → Folder...**

  The dialog box **Import Folder** is shown:

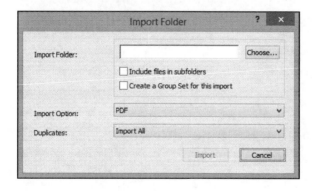

  3. Use [**Choose...**] to find the folder with the PDF collection.
  4. Select other options.
  5. Import with [**Import**].

Searching Text in PDF-files

EndNote X4 – X7 can search text in a PDF file using the normal Search Panel.

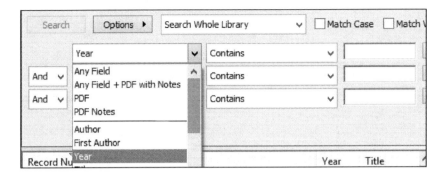

You can choose from *Any Field + PDF with Notes* or *PDF* or *PDF Notes*. The result, however, is always a number of shown references which means that you cannot easily find the searched word or term in the PDF-article. To find a specific word you need to open the article in the Tab Panel, the PDF viewer or using Acrobat Reader and make a new text search.

Renaming PDFs

Imported PDFs have usually nonsense-like names. Therefore such files are difficult to find when they are located in a common folder. Using the settings suggested on page 19 you can easily change names to more meaningful names.

♦ **Follow These Steps**
1   Highlight the records with PDFs you want to rename.
2   Go to **References → File Attachments → Rename PDFs...**

Renaming takes place instantly and is confirmed with:

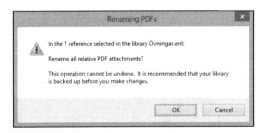

10. INSERTING CITATIONS IN THE TEXT

This is probably the most important feature in EndNote.

Your First Decision is deciding the position of the citation or citations. The position is defined by the current position of the cursor.

Your Second Decision is which citation or citations from the EndNote Library you want to insert.

This action may be carried out mainly in two ways:

♦ **Follow These Steps**

1 Open your Word manuscript.
2 Position the cursor where the citation shall be inserted.
3 Over to EndNote by going to
   EndNote X7 | Citations | Go to EndNote
   or key command **[Alt] + [1]**.
4 Select a reference in your Library with the pointer and a click. Several references are selected by pressing the **[Ctrl]**-key and clicking on each wanted reference. An interval of references is selected by pressing the **[Shift]**-key and a clicking on the first and the last reference in the interval.
5 The actual insert command can be made either from EndNote or from Word.
   From EndNote:
   Go to **Tools → Cite While You Write [CWYW] → Insert Selected Citation(s)**
   or key command **[Alt] + [2]**
   or the icon .
   From Word:
   Go to **EndNote X7 | Citations | Insert Citation → Insert selected Citation(s)**
   or key command **[Alt] + [2]**.
6 After the insertion of the citation or citations the software returns to Word provided the settings suggested on page 25 prevails.

If you need to return to Word from EndNote at any other situation the following options are available:

• **Tools → Cite While You Write [CWYW] → Go to Word Processor**
• Key command **[Alt] + [1]**
• Windows program selector **[Alt] + [Tab]**
• Windows program list

Our conclusion is that the easiest way to shift or toggle between Word and EndNote is by using the key command [**Alt**] + [**1**] that works from both applications.

Alternative inserting procedures are:

- Copy a reference from EndNote and paste into Word.
- Drag-and-drop from EndNote to Word
- From Word:
  Go to **EndNote X7 | Citations | Insert Citation**
  or key command [**Alt**] + [**7**]
  and this window is shown:

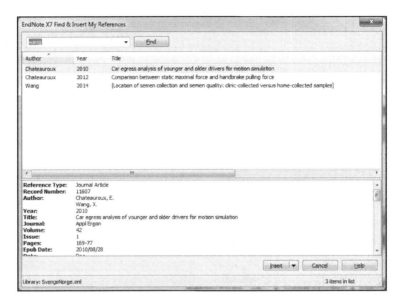

In the upper leftmost text box you type a search word (Author, word in the Title, Abstract or a Record Number) and then click [**Find**]. The result is shown as rows of references and you can select references you want to insert with [**Insert**].

The result can look like this:

har klickat på någon term i visningsformat Su

bektord {Vrkljan, 2011 #11709}. Du kan också

vudtema eller stänga av explode-funktionen

This is the unformatted citation (*Temporary Citation*). The surrounding bracket, { . . . } is called the *Temporary Citation Delimiter* and #11709 is the record number in the EndNote Library.

The type of bracket is defined under **Edit → Preferences**, section **Temporary Citations,** see page **22**. If your manuscript uses this type of bracket for other purposes in the text you might find reasons to change bracket.

The unformatted citation is not shown when using Instant Formatting. When you apply the settings on page 25 the unformatted citation is shown at each insertion.

Creating a bibliography is discussed on page 91.

11. INSERTING CITATIONS AS A FOOTNOTE

Your First Decision is deciding the position of the footnote with citation or citations. The position is defined by the current position of the cursor. Then you use the native footnote command in Word.

Your Second Decision is which citation or citations from the EndNote Library you want to insert.

This action may be carried out mainly in two ways:

♦   **Follow These Steps**

1   In Word: position the cursor where you want to insert the footnote.

2   Go to **References | Footnotes | Insert Footnote**
    or key command **[Ctrl]** + **[Alt]** + **[F]**.

The footnote window will open:

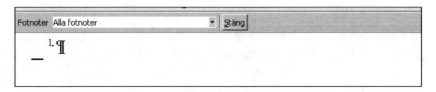

The insertion position of the citation is now determined.

3   Go to EndNote using
    EndNote X7 | Citations | Go to EndNote
    or key command **[Alt]** + **[1]**.

4   Select a reference in your Library with the pointer and a click. Several references are selected by pressing the **[Ctrl]**-key and clicking on each wanted reference. An interval of references is selected by pressing the **[Shift]**-key and a clicking on the first and the last reference in the interval.

5   The actual insert command can be made either from EndNote or from Word.
    From EndNote:
    Go to **Tools → Cite While You Write [CWYW] → Insert Citation(s)**
    or key command **[Alt]** + **[2]**
    or the icon ⬚.
    From Word:
    Go to **EndNote X7 | Citations | Insert Citations → Insert Selected Citation(s)**
    or key command **[Alt]** + **[2]**.

After the insertion of the citation or citations the software returns to Word provided the settings suggested on page 25 prevails.

Regarding shifting or toggling between Word and EndNote and

alternative commands for insertion of citations we refer to earlier sections of this book.

The result of this action with three footnotes is:

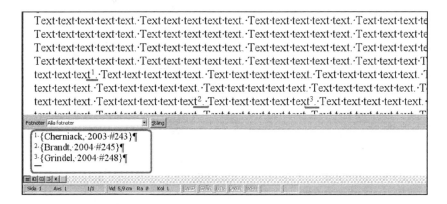

This is the unformatted citation *(Temporary Citation)*. The surrounding bracket, {.. .} is called the *Temporary Citation Delimiter* and **#243** is the record number in the EndNote Library.

About footnote settings in a Style, see page 116.

Creating a bibliography is discussed in Chapter 14, page 91.

12. INSERTING FIGURES AND TABLES

EndNote offers the option to archive graphic files (images, tables, figures) as records in an EndNote Library. Virtually any type of file format may be used as an attachment of such EndNote record, but this section deals with graphic files only. Once residing as an attachment of a record the graphics may be used similarly as any bibliographic record that can be inserted, formatted, edited and labeled in a Word manuscript. Each record can only store *one* graphics file and the field used for the attachment is the generic field *Image* which must be activated for the Reference Type in question. By default all reference types use the Image field. The field *Caption* is reserved for the label which will be displayed together with the graph in a Word manuscript.

Three reference types have been especially dedicated for storing such graphic files: Figure, Chart or Table, and Equation. However, any Reference Type may store a graphics file or any other file.

Reference Type Figure will create a listing of Figures with the in text citation (Figure 1), (Figure 2), (Figure 3) etc. and the text **List of Figures** when the output style has been set to create a list of figures at the end of the document.

All other reference types will create in-text citations (Table 1), (Table 2), (Table 3), etc. and the text **List of Tables** when the output style has been set to create a list of tables at the end of the document.

Creating a Record with a Graphic Attachment

First we need to create an EndNote record with a graphic file.

♦ **Follow These Steps**

1 Create a new record using **References → New Reference** or key command **[Ctrl]** + **[N]**

or the icon

or right.click in the Library windows and select **New Reference**.

2 Select Reference Type *Figure* from the drop-down list.

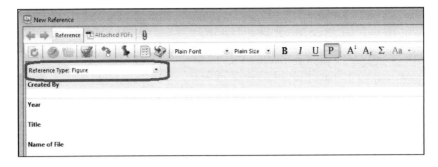

3   Go to **References → Figure → Attach Figure...**
or right-click in the reference window and select **Figure →
Attach Figure...**

4   Browse through folders and files until you have found the
graphics file you want to use.

5   Confirm with **[Open]**.

6   Type applicable text in the other fields of the EndNote
record especially in the *Caption* field because this text will
be displayed together with the graph in the Word
manuscript.

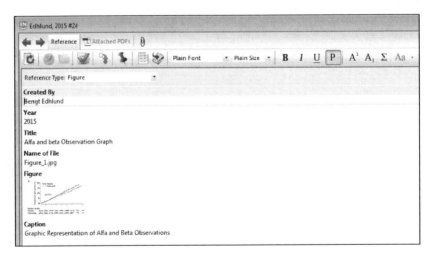

The graph is represented by a thumbnail or an icon in the Image
field. By clicking on the thumbnail or the icon the associated
application opens allowing editing to take place.

Each record can only store *one* graphics file. If you need to replace
the file then the command **Figure → Attach Figure...** inserts the
new file and the previous is replaced. If you need to delete a file
then mark the Image field of a record and apply the **[Delete]**-key.

Before the Reference window is closing EndNote asks the user to
save.

Where is the Attachment Stored?

During the described procedure the following takes place. The inserted file is *copied* and stored in a folder named [Library].DATA. This folder is created under the folder where the Library is residing.

Example: The current Library is MedLab.enl and resides in the folder ..\Libraries\ i.e. ..\ Libraries\MedLab.enl

The command **Figure → Attach Figure...** creates a copy of the file, Graph_01.jpg, which is located on our computer or located on a server in our local network.

The copy is called:

..\Libraries\MedLab.DATA\nnnnnnnnnnGraph_01.jpg

The nnnnnnnnnn represents an arbitrary ten or eleven digit prefix to the original file name. Each record creates an individual attachment and if two records should insert same graphics file one copy for each record is then created. When an attached graphics file is deleted from the Figure field with the [Del]-key then the source (the copy of the file) is also deleted.

When the command **File - Save a Copy...** is applied, then the program automatically creates not only a copy of the current library but also an attachment folder including all graphics or other attachments.

Also, when you need to merge libraries either by means of copying and pasting records or by means of importing one Library into another, see page 37, Merging Libraries, and then the attachment(s) will be automatically copied into the attachment folder of the target Library.

When moving or copying an EndNote Library by means of Windows Explorer, however, you must then remember to also copy the folder containing the attachments.

Finally, exporting records from a Library according to page 129 does not allow for the inclusion of any attachments, only the text contents of any field are included in the current style.

Inserting Graphs and Images in a Word Manuscript

The position of the in-text citation of a table or figure is determined by the position of the cursor. All operations are made from Word.

♦ **Follow These Steps**
   1   Position the cursor in the Word manuscript.
   2   Go to **EndNote X7 | Citations | Insert Citation → Insert Figure...** Then the following dialog box is shown:

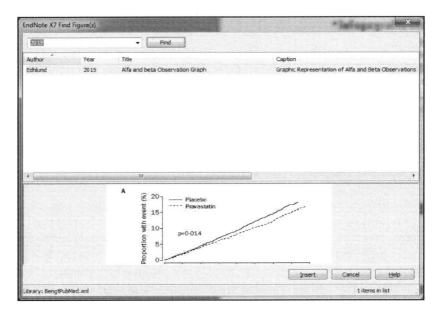

7 Type a search word in the text box then click [**Find**]. Such search is automatically limited to records with an attachment in the Figure field.

8 When the desired record shows then highlight the record and click the [**Insert**]-button.

The result may be like this:

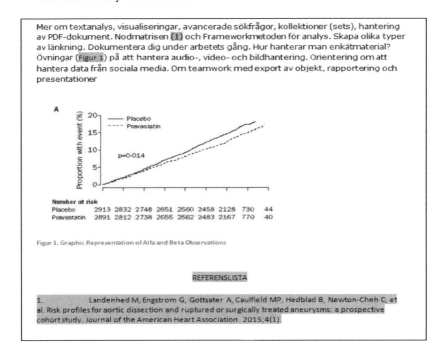

EndNote creates an in-text citation, a heading for the list of graphs, the graph itself and a caption label near the graph. The insertion of graphs is instantly formatted in conformity with the current Style. In the example above the Style is set to create the list of figures at the end of the document and the caption label below the graph.

Tables and Figures are listed separately and are displayed after the bibliography. In some instances the bibliography is placed after the List of Tables but before the List of Figures. If so, the bibliography can easily be moved with cut and paste and the bibliography will keep its position as long as unformatting of citations has not taken place.

After having inserted some citations, figures, and tables and then formatted the bibliography the document may look like this:

Mer om textanalys, visualiseringar, avancerade sökfrågor, kollektioner (sets), hantering av PDF-dokument. Nodmatrisen (1) och Frameworkmetoden (Tabell 1) för analys. Skapa olika typer av länkning. Dokumentera dig under arbetets gång. Hur hanterar man enkätmaterial? Övningar (Figur 1) på att hantera audio-, video- och bildhantering. Orientering om att hantera data från sociala media. Om teamwork med export av objekt, rapportering och presentationer

Tabell 1. Survey of Samples From Various Studies

	Placebo		Pravastatin		Hazard ratio (95% CI)	p*
	Total number	Number with event (%)	Total number	Number with event (%)		
Previous vascular disease†						
No	1654	200 (12·1)	1585	181 (11·4)	0·94 (0·77–1·15)	0·19
Yes	1259	273 (21·7)	1306	227 (17·4)	0·78 (0·66–0·93)	
Sex						
Female	1505	194 (12·9)	1495	186 (12·4)	0·96 (0·79–1·18)	0·13
Male	1408	279 (19·8)	1396	222 (15·9)	0·77 (0·65–0·92)	
LDL cholesterol (mmol/L)						
<3·41	978	158 (16·2)	972	137 (14·1)	0·88 (0·69–1·10)	0·69
3·41–4·11	1000	173 (17·3)	956	153 (16·0)	0·88 (0·70–1·10)	
>4·11	935	142 (15·2)	963	118 (12·3)	0·77 (0·60–0·98)	
HDL cholesterol (mmol/L)						
<1·11	1035	200 (19·3)	1016	132 (13·0)	0·64 (0·52–0·80)	0·0089
1·11–1·37	925	162 (17·5)	926	155 (16·7)	0·93 (0·75–1·16)	
>1·37	953	111 (11·6)	949	121 (12·8)	1·09 (0·84–1·41)	
Current smoker						
No	2108	348 (16·5)	2138	293 (13·7)	0·81 (0·69–0·95)	0·36
Yes	805	125 (15·5)	753	115 (15·3)	0·96 (0·74–1·24)	
History of hypertension						
No	1120	190 (17·0)	1092	162 (14·8)	0·85 (0·69–1·05)	0·91
Yes	1793	283 (15·8)	1799	246 (13·7)	0·84 (0·71–1·00)	
History of diabetes						
No	2593	414 (16·0)	2588	338 (13·1)	0·79 (0·69–0·91)	0·015
Yes	320	59 (18·4)	303	70 (23·1)	1·27 (0·90–1·80)	

*p for interaction values for heterogeneity of treatment across subgroups. †Any of stable angina or intermittent claudication, or stroke, transient ischaemic attack, myocardial infarction, arterial surgery, or amputation for vascular disease more than 6 months before study entry.

Table 3: Incidence of primary end point, according to subgroup

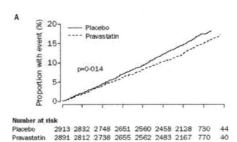

Figur 1. Graphic Representation of Alfa and Beta Observations

REFERENSLISTA

1.	Landenhed M, Engstrom G, Gottsater A, Caulfield MP, Hedblad B, Newton-Cheh C, et al. Risk profiles for aortic dissection and ruptured or surgically treated aneurysms: a prospective cohort study. Journal of the American Heart Association. 2015;4(1).

The editing options in a Word manuscript for figures and tables are: moving the position of the in-text label, deleting the in-text label (and the whole graph), and adding new graphs. Even though instant formatting always applies for figures and tables there is a need to refresh the lists of figures and tables after moving and deleting graphs. If the Style has been changed or modified a refresh will also be necessary.

Refresh is made with **EndNote X7 | Bibliography | Update Citations and Bibliography**.

Resizing and rotating[15] the graphs with normal Word commands is often necessary. Such resizing is restored after refresh of the figure and table lists.

If a record with a graphics file needs to be edited, like for example when the text in the caption field must be changed then the above refresh will not have an effect. In such cases the previous in-text label must be deleted and replaced and the modified record inserted.

The settings of the current Style determine the layout of tables and figures. The current Style can easily be opened by going to **Edit → Output Styles → Edit "current Style"**.

Choose **Figures** alt. **Tables** under **Figures & Tables** and the following options display:

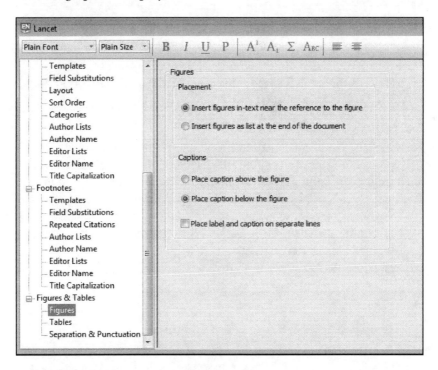

The option *Insert figures/tables in-text...* means that such graphs will be placed immediately after the paragraph where the in-text label has been placed. The text **List of Figures/Tables** will not display. Choose **Separation & Punctuation** under **Figures & Tables** and the following options will show:

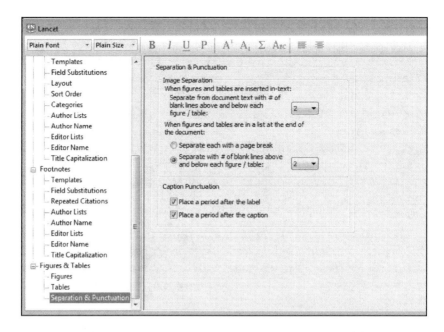

Each modification of a Style must be saved by EndNote with **File – Save As...** and when the Style has been saved with a new name you return to Word. Then finally you need to update the graphics according to the modified Style by using **EndNote X7 | Bibliography | Update Citation and Bibliography** or [**Alt**] + [**3**].

Convert Figures and Tables to Attachments

At times you could face a situation when you need to change status of figures and tables to become file attachments, which means that such items will be moved from the Figure field to the Attachments field.

♦ **Follow These Steps**

1 Highlight the reference(s) having figures and tables that need to be converted.

2 Go to **References → Figure → Convert Figures to File Attachments...**

13. INSERTING NOTES

At times there is a need of inserting notes which are not bibliographic references but are listed and numbered as in text citations and are sorted among the items of the bibliography. This feature can only be used by Word.

♦ **Follow These Steps**

1   From Word go to **EndNote X7 | Citations | Insert Citation →
    Insert Note...**

    or key command **[Alt] + [0]**.

This dialog box now appears:

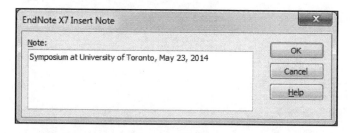

2   Type the note and confirm with **[OK]**.

The syntax for an unformatted note is:

```
{NOTE:Symposium at University of Toronto May 23,
2003}
```

Depending on the current Style the result after formatting may be like this:

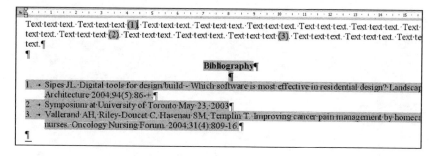

How to create a bibliography, see Chapter 14, page 91.

14. CREATING BIBLIOGRAPHIES

We have developed our recommendations on not applying Instant Formatting. There are many reasons behind:

- Computer power is utilized beyond out control with a risk of delays and other disturbances
- EndNote selects a Style often beyond our control
- The dialog box **EndNote X7 Configure Bibliography** is not shown

Formatting Bibliographies

Format Bibliography is the command that creates a bibliography in a Word manuscript.

♦ **Follow These Steps**
1 Open the Word documentet and the EndNote Library.
From Word:
2 Go to **EndNote X7 | Bibliography | Update Citations and Bibliography**.

A formatting takes place without showing the dialog box **Configure Bibliography**. The alternative is:
2 Key command **[Alt]** + **[3]**.

Then this dialog box with its two tabs is shown:

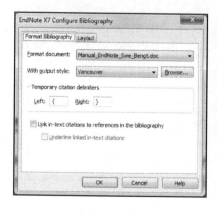 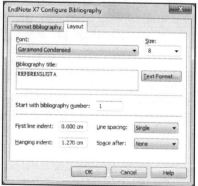

From EndNote:
2 Go to **Tools → Cite While You Write [CWYW] → Format Bibliography...**
or key command **[Alt]** + **[3]**.

Now we turn over to Word and the dialog box **Configure Bibliography** is shown as if we had used the key command **[Alt]** + **[3]** from Word.

This dialog box is important and easy to work with. The box confirms the name of the Word document and the current Style. When needed you can easily change Style or other settings.

The option *Link In-text Citations to references in the bibliography* will create a link from the citation to the reference in the bibliography.

The Layout tab can be used for the following modifications:

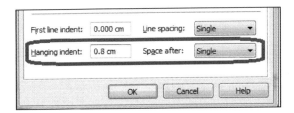

This setting means that the size of the hanging indent of the bibliography is more reasonable. We will also get somewhat more space between the references. The manuscript will become easier to read during a work session even if such settings may be without importance when finally published.

Handling Citations

Deleting, moving or adding citations must always be made in the text whether the citation is formatted or unformatted. Renewed formatting or refresh is made with the normal Format Bibliography command.

Deleting a citation is made with the same procedure as deleting any text, selecting and using the [**Del**]-key. It is a bit more complicated when you have a combined citation like [1–3] and one of the citations shall be deleted. More on this on page 109.

Edit the Reference in the EndNote Library

There are situations when you need to edit a reference in the EndNote Library outgoing from the citation in Word.

♦ **Follow These Steps**
  1   Position the cursor in the formatted citation.
  2   Go to **EndNote X7 | Citations | Edit Library Reference(s)** or key command [**Alt**] + [**5**].

The reference in the EndNote Library is opened and you can edit, save and format bibliography again.

Creating a Bibliography from Several Documents

In case you want to merge several documents into one after having written any number of chapters of a book or separate sections of an article you also want to create a common bibliography with citations from the various chapters or sections.

There are a few methods to choose from. Common for all methods is that all separate documents which are going to be merged must have *unformatted citations* before being merged.

For your main Word document, use any of the following methods:

- Use Word's Master Document feature.
- Insert file (note, *without link* to inserted document).
- Copy and paste from one document to another.

After merging all documents the usual **Format Bibliography** command will apply. Later you can add the contents from one more document which also needs to be *unformatted* before inserted or pasted into the main document.

Independent Bibliographies

An independent bibliography is a list of references that is not generated from citations in a paper but more self-generated. There are several occasions (literature list, order list, CV) when an independent bibliography is needed. EndNote offers various procedures, output styles and file formats.

The common principle for all procedures is that the current output style determines the format including text attributes, indenting, numbering, sorting etc.

Copy Formatted

EndNote has a unique feature called Copy Formatted. This command means that highlighted references are copied to the clipboard and formatted according to the current output style. In case several references are copied the sorting determined by the output style that prevails. If the sort order is Order of Appearance then sorting will be according to the order in which the references were highlighted.

- **Follow These Steps**
  1 Activate the current Library.
  2 Select an Output Style.
  3 Highlight selected reference(s).
  4 Go to **Edit → Copy Formatted**
     or key command **[Ctrl] + [K]**
     or right-click and select **Copy Formatted**.

The independent bibliography is now in the Windows clipboard and can be pasted into Word or any word processor, an e-mail, or virtually any other Windows application.

The Copy Formatted command cannot store paragraph attributes like indenting or line spacing. Text attributes, however, like bold, italic, underline and tabs are determined by the current output style.

Printing References

♦ **Follow These Steps**
1 Activate the current Library.
2 Select an Output Style.
3 Highlight selected reference(s).
4 Go to **File → Print**
   or key command **[Ctrl]** + **[P]**.
5 Confirm current printer settings.

When there is a need to print *only one reference* in accordance with the display of the Reference window including all displayed field names a special routine prevails which is *independent* from the current output style.

♦ **Follow These Steps**
1 Activate the current Library.
2 Open the selected reference.
3 Go to **File → Print**
   or key command **[Ctrl]** + **[P]**.
4 Confirm current printer settings.

15. SUBJECT BIBLIOGRAPHIES AND SUBJECT LISTS

A *Subject Bibliography* is an independent bibliography consisting of sections of literature references under separate headings and sorted according to certain criteria. The headings used are selected terms from the collection of references and can be any type of term such as authors, keywords, journals etc.

A *Subject List* is simply the list of selected headings but without the bibliographies. A subject list can be with or without subject term count which makes it possible to make simple frequency studies of selected references.

Practical uses of subject bibliographies are lists of journal abstracts, current awareness lists, subject indexes, or lists of holdings by category. When author names are used as subject headings this feature easily produces lists of literature for use in any CV.

The selection of records that shall be used when creating a Subject Bibliography or Subject List is determined as follows.

EndNote X7 uses the currently shown records when creating a Subject Bibliography or a Subject List That means the result of any search in a Library or the result of highlighting selected records followed by **References → Show Selected References**.

Here are two examples of a practical use of Subject Bibliographies and Subject Lists.

Example 1 – Subject Bibliography – Author's Bibliography

♦ **Follow These Steps**
  1 Open the current Library.
  2 Select the records to be included in the subject bibliography.
  3 Go to **Tools → Subject Bibliography...**
  4 Highlight *Author.*

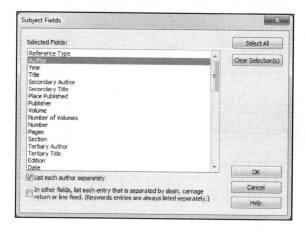

  5 Confirm with [**OK**].

6   In the Subject Terms highlight the requested author name(s). The default sort order is alphabetical. Sorting according to number of records (occurrence rate) is made by clicking on the [#**Records**]-button. Repeated click reverses the sort order.

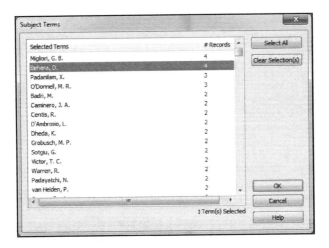

7   Confirm with [**OK**].

The result, depending on the settings, may be like this:

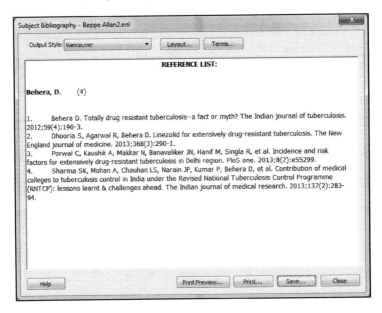

The [**Layout**]-button opens the dialog box **Subject Bibliography Setup** with four tabs for different settings.

The **References** tab:

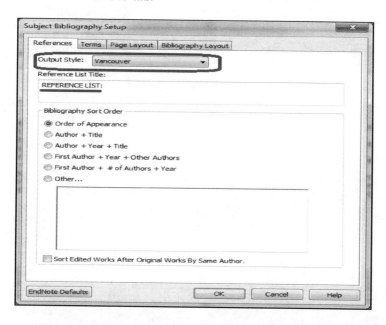

The current Style can be changed by selecting another Style from the drop-down list. The heading REFERENCE LIST has been typed in the Reference List Title text box.

The **Terms** tab:

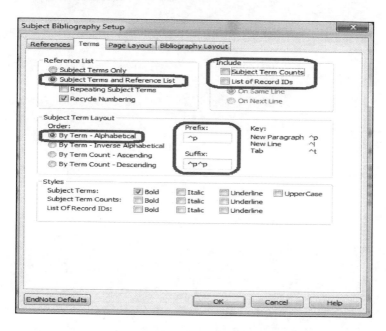

The choice is Subject Term and Reference List.

The **Page Layout** tab:

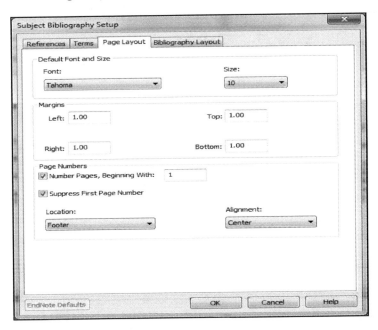

The default settings have been accepted.
The **Bibliography Layout** tab:

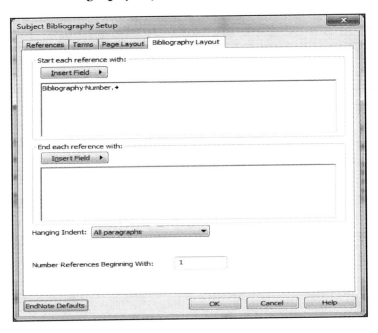

The default settings have been accepted.

Finally, when all settings for all tabs are accepted, confirm with [OK]. The settings are stored in EndNote until new changes are made. Restore EndNote default settings for individual tabs with the [**EndNote Defaults**]-button.

Example 2 – Subject List – Simple Frequency Study of Substances

♦ **Follow These Steps**

1 Open the current Library.
2 Select the records to be included in the subject bibliography.
3 Go to **Tools → Subject Bibliography...**
4 Highlight *Custom 3*, which in this example corresponds to the field *Substances*.
5 Check *In other fields ...* since this particular field is neither Author nor Keywords..

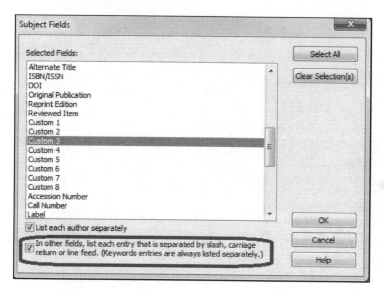

6 Confirm with [**OK**].

7   In the **Subject Terms** dialog box highlight the terms of
    interest for the current study.

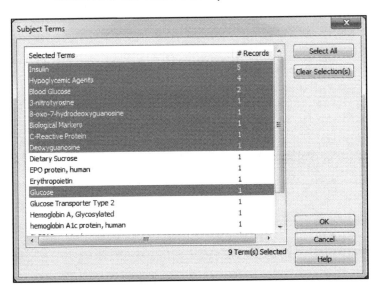

8   Confirm with [**OK**].
The result, depending on settings, may be like this:

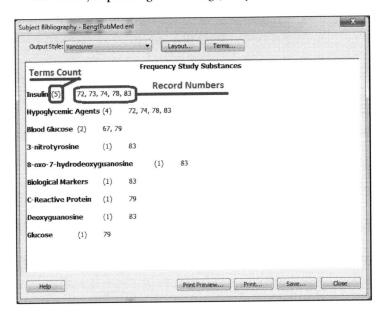

The [**Layout**]-button leads us to the Configure Subject
Bibliography dialog box and we comment on some settings specific
for this example.

The **References** tab:

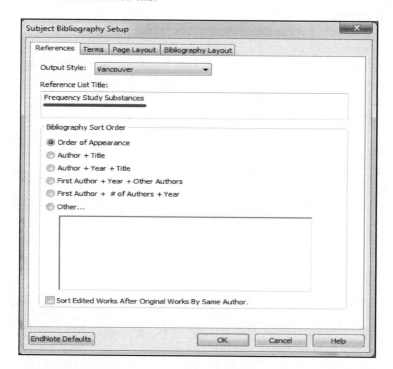

The **Terms** tab:

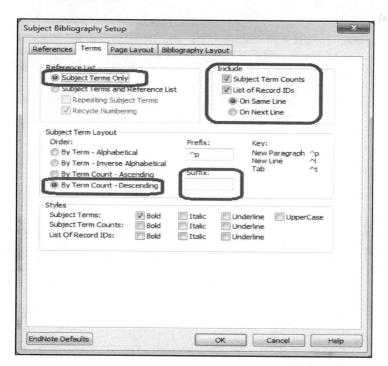

We selected Subject Terms Only, Subject Term Counts, and List of Record IDs. Sort order is by Term Count, Descending.

The default settings for the **Page Layout** and **Bibliography Layout** tabs have been accepted.

Finally, when all the settings for all tabs are selected, confirm with [**OK**]. The settings are stored in EndNote until new changes are made. Restore EndNote default settings for each individual tab with the [**EndNote Defaults**]-button.

- ♦ -

Finally, when the Subject Bibliography window displays an acceptable result, use the [**Print Preview...**], [**Print...**], or [**Save...**]-buttons for alternative outputs.

16. EDITING STYLES

The Output Styles in EndNote are proprietary files holding many different settings that together create the different output formats. These files have the file extension *.ENS for EndNote Style. EndNote is delivered with a large number (more than 1000) of prepared output styles. These styles differ in terms of their function and can be divided into two different groups: The *bibliographic formats* representing author instructions from a certain publisher or journal and the *utility formats* that can be used for printout, easy reading, document ordering, or export of data. EndNote incorporates all necessary tools to edit or create new such output styles.

The instrument to find, select, edit and mark-favorite styles is called the Style Manager and is described below.

Cases may occur when you cannot find one particular Style in EndNote's standard collection. This collection is continuously being expanded with new styles and the latest complete collection is available known as the Style Finder:
`http://endnote.com/downloads/styles`

Searching for a particular style which does not appear in your standard style collection or the Style Finder need not be a big problem. One initial issue is to find the required format described in a clear-cut way. There are several web-sites supporting author instructions.

Furthermore, it is worthwhile actually studying the details of the citations and the bibliography of an article from the journal in which you intend to publish your article. Also when you use some of EndNote's standard styles we suggest you verify the output style with an article as minor deviations and imperfections may occur. Even if the number of variants seem to be overwhelming, a great number of Styles are in fact identical (or nearly identical), even if they carry individual file names.

Using the Preview option of the Style Manager as described on page 112 is useful when you search for a style which is as near your need as possible. Simply open the Style Manager, select the *Preview* option, highlight a certain style and browse with the up or down arrow keys until you find a useful style. If you are lucky then the style could be used as is, otherwise you can modify according to the instructions that follow.

In this section we will give some examples of a few basic principles in editing. Some of the most common minor modifications of Styles are:

- Creating a Hanging Indent
- Changing the in-text citation from parentheses (..) to brackets [..]
- Changing the Title to **Bold**
- Changing the Journal Name to *Italic*
- Deleting the issue number

The Style Manager

First we need to choose some favorites among Styles.

♦ **Follow These Steps**
1 Go to **Edit → Output Styles → Open Style Manager...**
2 Search for your favorites with the [**Find by**]-button, and search for example Medicine, then search Vancouver.
3 Check the small box to the left.

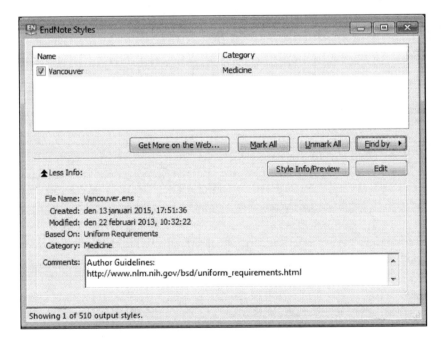

4 Search your next favorite and check again.
5 Close the Style Manager with the cross in the upper right-hand corner.

Before you close the Style Manager you can easily verify which favorites you have selected by using the [**Find by**]-button and then *Favorites*.

When the Style Manager is closed the list of favorites is also available on the drop-down list on the tool bar:

Opening a Style for editing can be made in two ways. The Style Manager is one instrument for doing so. When the Style Manager is open highlight the requested Style and apply the [**Edit**]-button. We will use the Style Vancouver to make the mentioned minor modifications. When Vancouver is the current Style in the dropdown list, there is also a shortcut to edit Vancouver:

♦ **Follow These Steps**
1   Go to **Edit → Output Styles → Edit "Vancouver"**.
2   Create a copy of Vancouver with **File → Save As...**
3   Name the new Style for example `vancouver_mod`.
4   Save with [**Save**].

In case of misspelling or an editing mistake you can use the undo function **Edit → Undo** or [**Ctrl**] + [**Z**], to return to an earlier saved version. As soon as a modification is saved the undo function is off.

Introducing Hanging Indent

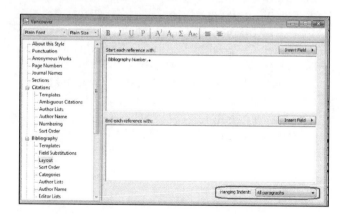

♦ **Follow These Steps**
1   Open the Style.
2   Go to **Bibliography → Layout**.
3   Select *All paragraphs* from the **Hanging Indent: drop-down list**.
4   Save the modified settings.

Modifying Citations

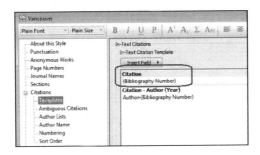

♦ **Follow These Steps**

1 Open the Style.
2 Go to **Citations → Templates**.
3 Modify directly in the text box by replacing parentheses (..) with brackets [..].
4 Save the modified settings.

Note, that the second line is an alternative instruction to be used when you edit the citation, see page 109

Changing Title to Bold and Journal Name to Italic

The edit mode of **Bibliography → Templates** displays a separate instruction for each existing reference type. The instruction consists of text elements, field elements, and special symbols. When writing or editing such instructions all reference types are available as a list from the button [**Reference Types**] and as a list with field elements and special symbols from the button [**Insert Field**]. The special symbols are explained on page 112. Should an instruction for a certain reference type be missing in the list of styles there is a fallback in the form of reference type *Generic* when formatting takes place.

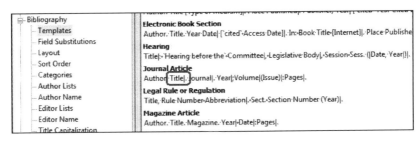

- **Follow These Steps**
  1. Open the Style.
  2. Go to **Bibliography → Templates**.
  3. Highlight *Title* in the Journal Article instruction box.
  4. Apply text attribute **Bold**.
  5. Highlight *Journal* in the Journal Article instruction box.
  6. Apply text attribute *Italic*.
  7. Save settings.

Synonyms for Journal Names

In certain instances there are author instructions that require alternative journal names i.e. synonyms to those journal names that are found in the records of an EndNote Library. For example the EndNote records may use *N Engl J Med* whereas the instruction requires the format *N. Engl. J. Med.* or *New England Journal of Medicine*.

The solution is to import and use supporting Journal Term Lists as mentioned on page 126. Having imported such term lists the Style must then be modified.

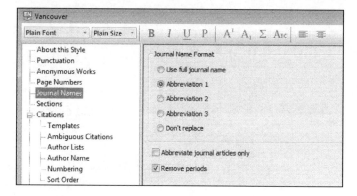

- **Follow These Steps**
  1. Open the Style for editing.
  2. Go to **Journal Names**.
  3. Select the alternative that corresponds to the columns of the term list for journal names.
  4. Save settings.

Deleting the Issue Number

Electronic Book Section			
Author. Title. Year Date| [`cited `Access Date]|. In: Book Title [Internet]|. Place Published|: Publisher|. Edition.|		

Hearing
Title|. Hearing before the Committee|. Legislative Body|. Session Sess. (|Date, Year|)|.

Journal Article
Author. Title|. Journal|. Year|; Volume| (Issue)|:Pages|.

Legal Rule or Regulation
Title, Rule Number Abbreviation|. Sect. Section Number (Year)|.

Magazine Article
Author. Title. Magazine. Year|·Date|:Pages|.

◆ **Follow These Steps**
1 Open the Style for editing.
2 Go to **Bibliography → Templates**.
3 Highlight *(Issue)* in the Journal Article instruction box.
4 Delete with **Edit → Clear** or the [**Del**]-key.
5 Save settings.

Finally, in order to make these modifications have an effect on the citations and the bibliography in the manuscript, refresh is made with the normal Format Bibliography command.

Edit & Manage Citations

♦ **Follow These Steps**

1 Position the cursor in the formatted citation.

2 Go to **EndNote X7 | Citations | Edit & Manage Citations**
or [Alt] + [6]
or right-click and select **More**.

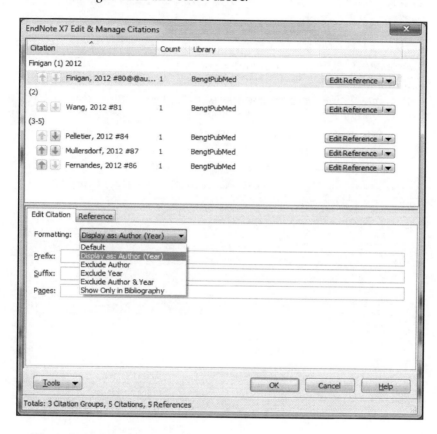

The **Edit Reference** drop-down list has the following options:
- Edit Library Reference
- Find References Updates
- Remove Citations
- Insert Citation
- Update from My Library...

If a citation is for multiple references, like (3–5) above, then you can change the internal order with the up and down arrows or using the other options. You may also individually change a citation by using the **Edit Citation** tab and select the *Display as:<..>* at the **Formatting** drop-down list. This option is the second alternative for the Citation when editing a Style which was mentioned on page 106.

The **Tools** drop-down list has the following options:
- Update Citations and Bibliography (see page 91)
- Configure Bibliography (see page 91)
- Export Traveling Library (see page 119)

The **Reference** tab shows the highlighted reference with all its fields directly from the Library. This dialog box also shows Libraries used for each reference.

Prefix and Suffix in a Citation

Sometimes there is a need to add a prefix or a suffix to an individual citation.

Example: The formatted citation is [4]. The author wants to add a prefix and a suffix so that the citation will become:
`[See especially 4, pages 24-25]`

◆ **Follow These Steps**
1   Position the cursor in the formatted citation.
2   Go to **EndNote X7 | Citations | Edit & Manage Citations**
    or **[Alt] + [6]**
    or right-click and select **More**.

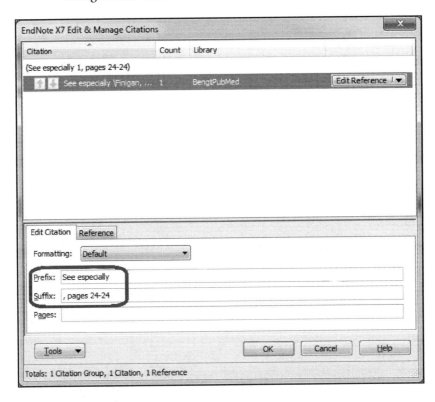

3   Type the required prefix and suffix in the respective text boxes. Consider spaces if needed.

4   Confirm with [**OK**].

The immediate result is of this operation is the temporary citation:

`{See especially\Finigan, 2012 #80, pages 24-25}`

And after formatting (refresh) the result becomes:

`[See especially Finigan, 4, pages 24-25]`

Cited Pages

EndNote offers the possibility of using a special virtual field, Cited Pages, when creating a Style. The Cited Pages field can only be used in the Citation Template and the Footnote Template. This field may be used as if it was any other field. Text attributes may also be applied.

The information in this field however is not in the EndNote Library, but it the Word document and individual for each citation. The Cited Pages information is inserted with:

EndNote X7 | Citation(s) | Edit & Manage Citation(s) or **[Alt] + [6]:**

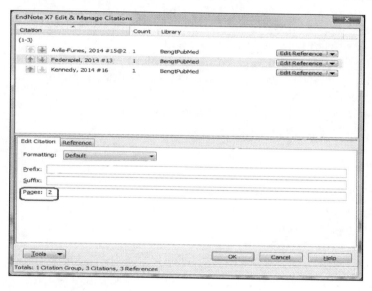

For example, let's assume we have the following instruction in the Citation Template of a particular Style:

(Author, Year‚₀see₀page^^pages`₀Cited Pages)

Depending on what we type in the **Pages:** text box we will have the following alternative results of a formatted citation:

- Typed in the text box **Pages:**
  - upon formatting: `(Kallstrom, 2004)`
- Typed in the text box **Pages:** 2
  - upon formatting: `(Kallstrom, 2004, see page 2)`
- Typed in the text box **Pages:** 24-56
  - upon formatting: `(Kallstrom, 2004, see pages 24-56)`

Special Symbols used in Styles

With the previous example we list some comments on special symbols used in Styles:

| Forced Separation (vertical bar) is used for unlinking elements in a template instruction. That means if a referred field is empty then linked or adjacent text elements will be omitted up to the Forced Separation character.

o Link Adjacent text means that when a field is not empty then the adjacent text elements will display.

^ Singular/Plural between two text elements means that the first element is used when the singular applies and the second when the plural applies.

~ surrounding a word implies a text element in contrast to a field element should a confusion occur.

→ Tab

¶ End-of-Paragraph.

Testing a Modified Output Style

There are two ways to view the effect of a modified style on a record. It is quite normal to modify and view repeatedly before the required result is achieved.

The first preview option is already available in the Tab Panel and the Preview tab. As soon as you select a reference you will see the effect of your current Style under modification:

The Style Manager also has a preview function. Choose *Style Info/Preview* from the drop-down list, highlight the style you need to examine and the result of three default references (the first is a Journal Article) are displayed in the lower window. The up and down arrows of the keyboard are used to scroll the list of styles.

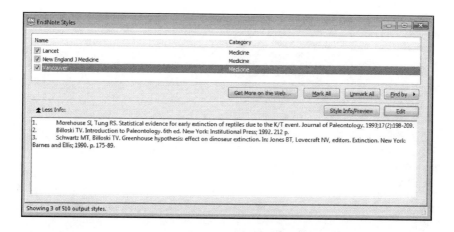

More on Indents, Margins, Tabs, and Text Attributes

This section is a result of frequently asked questions in connection with paragraph formatting of bibliographies. The section therefore takes up certain questions and the best suggested solutions.

Problem 1 – Too long a Tab Distance

This style requires no hanging indent but a tab after the bibliography number. The tab distance is far too long.

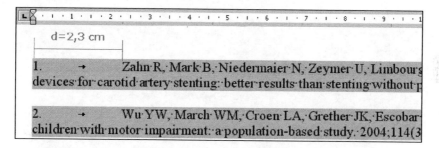

Solution: Word's default tab stops (usually 2.3 cm) is reflected in the paragraph formatting. To change (normally decrease) this distance go to Word: **Home | Paragraph → [Tabs...]** and change the default tab stops to *0.5 cm*. Confirm with **[OK]**. The modification will have an immediate effect.

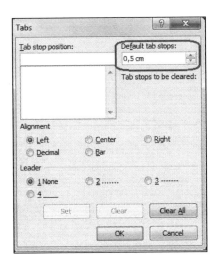

Problem 2 – A Tab precedes the Bibliography Number

This style requires no hanging indent but there is a tab before and a tab after the bibliography number. Both tab distances are far too long.

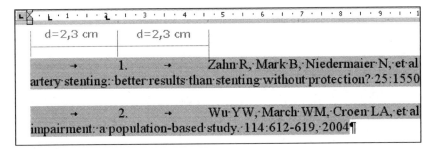

Solution: In EndNote, open the current style for editing, see page 104. Select the section **Bibliography → Layout**, delete the unwanted tab symbol, save the style, and refresh with the Format Bibliography command. Modify the standard distance for tabs according to the solution for Problem 1.

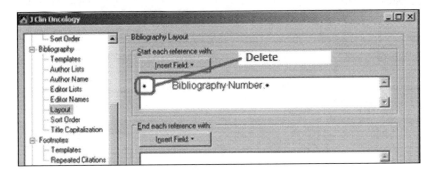

Problem 3 - Too long a Hanging Indent

This style has a hanging indent which is far too long.

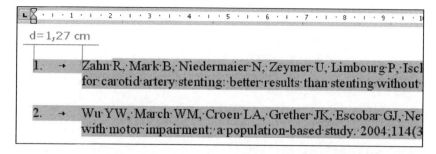

Solution: The standard distance for a hanging indent for new documents is 1.27 cm and is set in the dialog box **EndNote X7 Configure Bibliography**, the **Layout** tab and **Hanging indent**. Apply a new value, for example *0.8 cm* which will be saved for the current document. Confirm with [**OK**].

Problem 4 - The Complete Bibliography is Bold

The complete bibliography is bold after formatting but only a few or none text elements according to the current style should be bold!

> ▪ **REFERENCES**¶
> ▪ ¶
> ▪ **1** → **Zahn·R,·Mark·B,·Niedermaier·N,·et·al.·Embolic·protection·devices· for·carotid·artery·stenting:·better·results·than·stenting·without· protection?·2004;25:1550-1558.**¶
> ▪ **2** → Wu·YW,·March·WM,·Croen·LA,·Grether·JK,·Escobar·GJ,· Newman·TB.·Perinatal·stroke·in·children·with·motor·impairment:· a·population-based·study.·2004;114:612-619.¶

Solution: When a bibliography is formatted for the first time the paragraph template from the last paragraph in the document applies but it uses fonts, size and tabs from paragraph template Normal. This implies that text attributes (bold, italic, superscript, subscript etc.) are inherited from this last paragraph. In other words if the last paragraph in the document is the title **REFERENCES** with attribute bold the whole bibliography will be bold the first time formatting is applied. If this is the case the whole bibliography must be unformatted with Unformat Citation(s). Then a new paragraph must be created and this new paragraph must be cleansed from all undesired attributes. Finally refresh with Format Bibliography.

Adding and Merging Citations

Adding a citation to an existing citation is very easy.

♦ **Follow These Steps**

1 Position the cursor immediately before or after the existing citation without space.

2 Insert the new citation.

The immediate result is:

`[3]{Finigan, 2012 #80}`

And after having formatted (refresh) the final result may look like this: `[3,4]`.

About Citations in Footnotes

A Style determines how a citation in a footnote is formatted. In the open style mode **Footnotes → Templates** may be chosen. The prime choice is **Format citations in footnotes**: drop-down list. The options are:

- Same as bibliography
- Same as citations
- Using footnote format

The two first options require no other settings other than the existing formatting instructions under the respective headings. The third option, Using Footnote Format, requires a complete formatting instruction in the Footnote Template textbox. The special field Cited Pages may be used, see page 111.

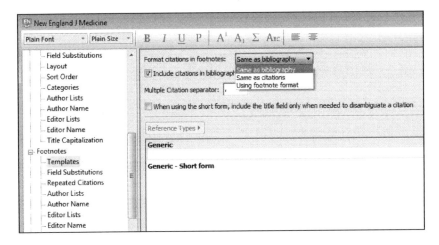

The section **Footnotes → Repeated Citations** offers settings for a short form of the repeated footnote. This is valid for all three options of the Footnote Template mentioned above. The short form includes only the Author names without initials. Title alt. Short Title can be added to the short form.

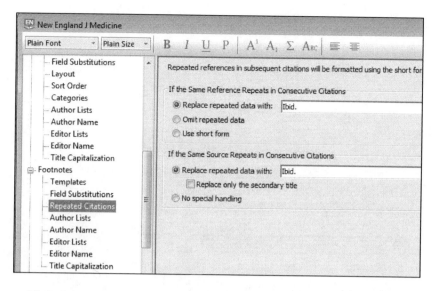

If the same reference or same source is repeated in consecutive footnotes there are detailed options on how to format the footnote citation.

Unformat Citations

The command Unformat Citation(s) means that all citations in the document or certain citations are becoming unformatted citations. This command is only available from Word.

When you need to unformat all citations in the document:

- **Follow These Steps**
  1. Position the cursor anywhere in the document without any citation being selected.
  2. Go to **EndNote X7 | Bibliography | Convert Citations and Bibliography → Convert to Unformatted Citations** or key command **[Alt] + [4]**.

When you need to unformat a selected citation:

- **Follow These Steps**
  1. Select the citation you want to unformat.
  2. Go to **EndNote X7 | Bibliography | Convert Citations and Bibliography → Convert to Unformatted Citations** or key command **[Alt] + [4]**.

17. TRAVELING LIBRARY

A Traveling Library is a function that stores bibliographic data from the inserted references in a Word document in the form of embedded field codes. The Abstract, Notes and Image fields are not included in a Traveling Library.

The first time a citation is formatted the corresponding Library must be open. Later when any reformatting takes place the bibliographic data is captured from the Traveling Library. After unformatting citation(s) the EndNote Library needs to be open before formatting can take place again.

This means that it is possible to send a formatted document to a computer that has installed EndNote but not the same Library. This computer may even re-format and use another Style. But as soon as the document is unformatted and saved then an open Library with these references must be open in order to format again.

The embedded field codes may be exported from a Word document to an EndNote Library with all bibliographic data. Such a Traveling Library will not have the same record numbers as the originally used Library which is why it cannot be fully used with the document until all earlier citations have been replaced with records from the Traveling Library.

From Word:

♦ **Follow These Steps**
1   Go to **EndNote X7 | Tools | Export to EndNote → Export Traveling Library**
     or key command [**Alt**] + [**8**].

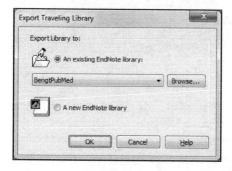

2   Finally, select a new or an existing Library for the export.
3   Confirm with [**OK**].

From EndNote:

- **Follow These Steps**
    1 Go to **Tools → Cite While You Write [CWYW] → Import Traveling Library...**
      or key command **[Alt] + [8]**.

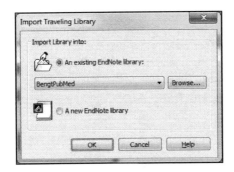

2 Finally, select a new or an existing Library for the import.
3 Confirm with **[OK]**.

Sending a Word-document between Users

At times there is a need to send documents between users for proofreading, adding comments, or as information. The best format to use depends on how the parties work together and if same version of EndNote and respectively Word are used. The best guarantee for a reliable exchange of information is when all parties use the same version of both software. It is recommended but not imperative that both the Word-document and the EndNote Library travel together and are updated by one particular user at a time.

If the receiver uses EndNote X7 but not the same EndNote Library as the sender it is quite safe to send the formatted Word-document and benefit from the simplicity of the Traveling Library.

Should a proofreader, who does not use EndNote, edit the text it is far safer to send a Word-document without field codes as described for the Publisher's Copy on page 121. Changes made should be inserted in the master document with great care. We suggest using the Word features under **Tools → Track Changes → Compare Documents** or under **Insert → Comment**.

Compatibility between Documents

User of different versions of EndNote must observe the following aspects of a Traveling Library. Different versions of Word are not critical when working with Traveling Libraries, but different versions of EndNote may sometimes cause problems.

18. REMOVING FIELD CODES

When you submit your paper to the publisher, the Word document must be formatted with the EndNote's Format Bibliography command. It is also highly recommended that the field codes be converted to text. If the field codes are left open in a computer that does not have EndNote, the document could easily be corrupted or be difficult to import by the publisher's word processor.

In Word:

♦ **Follow These Steps**

1   Go to **EndNote X7 | Bibliography | Convert Citations & Bibliography → Convert to Plain Text**.

EndNote will remind you to save the *Working Copy* and creates a new copy of the document where the field codes from EndNote have been converted to normal text. This copy of the document is usually referred to as *Publisher's Copy*. After the Remove Field Codes command you will need to save the new copy with a new name with the **Save As...** command. This copy cannot be restored for further EndNote editing. In case you need to edit your manuscript you must return to the Working Copy.

Field shading according to recommended settings on page 24 will make it easier during the working session to immediately recognize the Working Copy and Publisher's Copy respectively.

The working copy, formatted and with field shading:

Text text text text. (1) Text text text text. Text text text text. Text text text text. Text text text text. Text text text text. Text text text text. Text text text text. Text text text text. Text text text text. Text text text text. (2) Text text text text. Text text text text. Text text text text. (3) Text text text text. Text text text text. Text text text text. Text text text text. Text text text text. ¶
¶

REFERENCES¶
¶

1. → Ververeli K, Chipps B. Oral corticosteroid-sparing effects of inhaled corticosteroids in the treatment of persistent and acute asthma. Ann Allergy Asthma Immunol 2004;92(5):512-22.¶

2. → Kallstrom TJ. Evidence-based asthma management. Respir Care 2004;49(7):783-92.¶

3. → Patel PH, Welsh C, Foggs MB. Improved asthma outcomes using a coordinated care approach in a large medical group. Dis Manag 2004;7(2):102-11.¶

The publisher's copy with field codes converted to text:

Text·text·text·text.·(1)·Text·text·text·text.·Text·text·text·text.·Text·text·text·text.·Text·text·text·text.·Text·text·text·
text.·Text·text·text·text.·Text·text·text·text.·Text·text·text·text.·Text·text·text·text.·Text·text·text·text.·Text·text·text·
text.·Text·text·text·text.·(2)·Text·text·text·text.·Text·text·text·text.·Text·text·text·text.·(3)·Text·text·text·text.·Text·
text·text·text.·Text·text·text·text.·Text·text·text·text.·Text·text·text·text.¶
¶

REFERENCES¶
¶

1. → Ververeli·K,·Chipps·B.·Oral·corticosteroid-sparing·effects·of·inhaled·corticosteroids·in·the·treatment·of·
persistent·and·acute·asthma.·Ann·Allergy·Asthma·Immunol·2004;92(5):512-22.¶

2. → Kallstrom·TJ.·Evidence-based·asthma·management.·Respir·Care·2004;49(7):783-92.¶

3. → Patel·PH,·Welsh·C,·Foggs·MB.·Improved·asthma·outcomes·using·a·coordinated·care·approach·in·a·large·
medical·group.·Dis·Manag·2004;7(2):102-11.¶

Manually Removing Field Codes

Word's generic command for removing field codes, [**Ctrl**] + [**6**], may at certain occasions be an alternative method.

♦ **Follow These Steps**
1 Highlight the fields you want to unlink, or if all text, then use key command [**Ctrl**] + [**A**].
2 Unlink with key command [**Ctrl**] + [**6**].
3 Go to **File** → **Save As...** and determine name and file location of your unlinked document.

This is the preferred procedure when using the EndNote's Word templates as described in Chapter 21, page 139.

A few important considerations specific for this method are:

- If your document contains *footnotes* with field codes that you want to unlink, then you need to highlight the document body and the footnote window separately and do the unlinking for each window.
- Unlinking a whole document with this method removes *all field codes* even such field codes that are not created by EndNote, for example cross-references, tables of contents, indexes etc..
- Embedded or linked objects like objects from Excel Worksheets or Charts applying layout mode *In line with text* will be unlinked and converted to Picture objects (Windows Metafile) which is the preferred format when sending a manuscript to a publisher.

19. TERM LISTS

EndNote has the capacity to create term lists built up from certain field(s) and related to an individual Library. Term lists are alphabetically sorted lists with eliminated duplicates. EndNote is by default prepared to create term lists for Authors, Keywords, and Journals. Term Lists can also be imported from external sources and exported as text files for use in other applications..

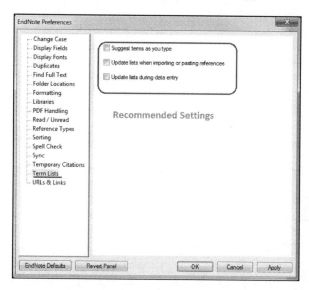

By factory default Term Lists Preferences are set for suggesting terms and automatic update. We recommend however, that the preferences are set for manual handling of term lists.

♦   **Follow These Steps**
1   Go to **Edit → Preferences**.
2   Choose section **Term Lists**.
3   Uncheck all three options.
4   Confirm with [**OK**].

The reason why we recommend manual update of term lists is that term lists can unnecessarily oversize the libraries for those who do not use term lists. Also automatic update does not reduce term lists when records are deleted, which may cause term lists to grow out of control.

Term lists have import and export options.

A term list of special significance is the Journals Term List, which has four columns with alternative terms, or synonyms.

Creating a New Term List

In certain circumstances there is a need for special term lists, e.g. for chemicals and substances.

♦ **Follow These Steps**
    1   Open the EndNote Library for which you need the term list.
    2   Go to **Tools → Define Term Lists...**
        or key command [**Ctrl**] + [**4**].

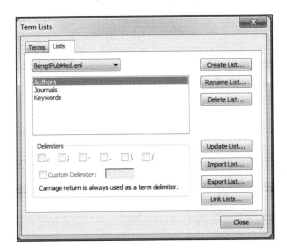

    3   Use the [**Create List...**]-button.

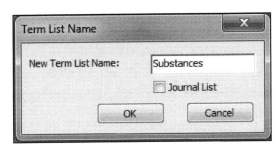

    4   Type a new name for the new term list, e.g. Substances.
    5   Confirm with [**OK**] followed by [**OK**] in the Term Lists-window.

Linking the Term List to Certain Fields

◆ **Follow These Steps**

1 Go to **Tools → Link Term Lists...**
   or key command **[Ctrl] + [3]**.

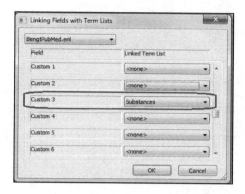

2 Scroll the list until the field **Custom 3** is shown in the left column.

3 Select a term list, *Substances,* from the drop-down list. If required, more than one field can be linked to a term list.

4 Confirm with **[OK]**.

Manual Update of Term List

We suggest the manual update of term lists. To ensure that the term list only accommodates terms from existing records the list needs to be set to zero and then updated.

◆ **Follow These Steps**

1 Open the term list.
2 Select all terms with key command **[Ctrl] + [A]**.
3 Delete all terms with the **[Delete Term]**-button.
4 Update with the **[Update List...]**-button from the **Lists** tab.

5 Confirm with **[OK]**.

Opening a Term List

All term lists are accessible under **Tools → Open Term Lists → <name> Term List**. It is convenient to select the name of the term list with the pointer.

The Term List *Autors* is opened:

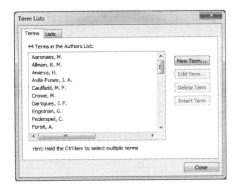

Importing Term Lists

When there is a need to use synonyms or alternative journal names an external term list may be imported. Please note, that the Journal Term List is a four column list prepared for a set of synonyms per row.

◆ **Follow These Steps**

1   Go to **Tools → Open Term Lists**.
2   Select *Journals Term List.*
3   Use the **Term**s tab and highlight all terms with **[Ctrl]** + **[A]**.
4   Delete all terms with the **[Delete Term]**-button.
5   Use the **List** tab and highlight Journals.
6   Click the **[Import List...]**-button.
7   Select appropriate Term List such as one residing in the Term Lists folder.
8   Confirm with **[Open]**.

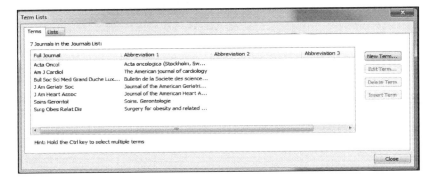

9   Close with med [**Close**].

This option should be used only when needed and in combination with Styles set for alternative journal names. See page 107. Please note, that such term lists are specific for each Library. If several libraries are used for Styles set for alternative journal names then each Library must import such term lists. Large term lists makes the size of each Library grow and should therefore not be used unless really needed.

Searching with Term Lists

♦   **Follow These Steps**

1   Go to **References** → **Search References...**
      or key command [**Ctrl**] + [**F**]
      or right-click and select **Search References...**
      and the search form will display.

2   Select the *Custom 2* field and place the cursor in the text box.

3   Use key command [**Ctrl**] + [**1**] and the linked term list will automatically open.

4   Highlight a term with the pointer or type the initial character (or, typing quickly, the two or even three initial characters) of the wanted term, which will then be highlighted.

5   Double-click the term or apply [**Insert Term**] and the term will be pasted into the text box.

6   When required, add more terms or search strings in the forthcoming text boxes of the search form.

7   Click the [**Search**]-button or simply the [**Enter**]-key.

Creating Records with Term Lists

♦ **Follow These Steps**

1 Create a new reference with **References → New Reference** or key command **[Alt] + [N]**
or right-click and select **New Reference** and the empty New reference window will display:

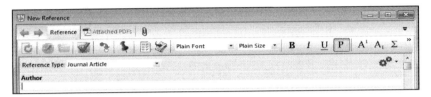

2 Position the cursor in the Author field.
3 Use key command **[Ctrl] + [1]** and the linked term list (Author) will open automatically

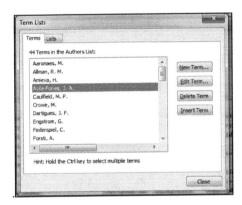

4 Highlight the term(s) you intend to insert and double-click or click **[Insert Term]**.

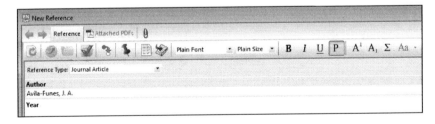

You may then proceed to other linked fields and apply the same procedure.

20. DATABASE PRODUCTION TOOLS

EndNote has the capacity of not only to import and capture data from external databases but also to build databases of its own. This will be necessary for many users who need references for manuscript writing but do not have access to databases with convenient data transfer capacity to reference handling software.

There are also many occasions when data imported or captured from external sources will need some cleaning up due to imperfections in original data or import procedures.

In some cases third party software like Microsoft Excel or FileMaker may be of valuable assistance for the production of databases. In those cases a tab delimited text file is often the format that makes data transfer between EndNote and a third party software possible

Exporting Data - General

The export function in EndNote is characterized by the following:
- Exported references are the currently viewed records
- The current Output Style determines the structure of the file
- File formats options are text file, RTF, HTML, XML

♦ **Follow These Steps**
1   Activate the current Library.
2   Select a suitable Output Style, e.g. *Tab Delimited*.
3   If all records in the Library will be exported apply **References → Show All References** and proceed to 5 otherwise highlight the records you intend to export.
4   Go to **References → Show Selected References**.
5   Go to **File → Export...**
6   Determine name and file location and file format e.g. text file.

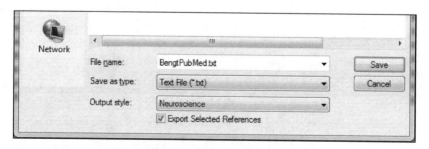

7   Confirm with [**Save**].

Available file types are Text (*.txt), Rich Text (*.rtf), HTML (*.htm) and XML (*.xml). Exported data are, except for XML, dependent of the current Style. There are a number of Styles especially designed for various export requirements. You will find those Styles under the category *Export* in the Style Manager. If *Export Selected References* is checked only the selected references will be exported otherwise all shown references.

Exported data can be imported by a third party software able to import tab delimited text files. Be aware, that a tab delimited text file cannot be re-imported to EndNote until it has been re-structured according to the rules specified later in this book.

Exporting Data to Excel

This section refers to the Style *Tab Delimited ENX2 Excel.ens* and the Excel template *EndNoteX2.xlt*. These items can be ordered free-of-charge by readers of this book. Just send a mail to sales@formkunskap.com.

When the need arises to export data to Excel for re-structuring or modification some special considerations are necessary.

♦ **Follow These Steps**

1 Activate the current Library.

2 Select the special Style, *Tab Delimited ENX2 Excel.ens* for EndNote X2 or later.

3 Replace all line feeds in the Library with semicolon using **Edit → Find and Replace** or **[Qtrl] + [R]** and type **Find: [Ctrl] + [Enter]** or use **[Insert Special]** and select *Carriage return* and **Replace with: ; [Space]**.

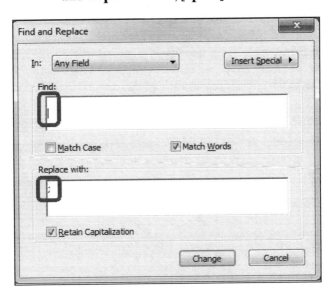

4 Confirm with **[Change]**.

5   Highlight the references you want to export. If you want to export the whole Library, use key command for Show All, **[Ctrl]** + **[M]** then for Highlight All **[Ctrl]** + **[A]**.

6   Use key command for Copy Formatted, **[Ctrl]** + **[K]**.

7   Open Excel and click on the Office Button and go o New and select My Templates. Under the **EndNote** tab, select the template *EndNoteX2.xlt* for EndNote X2 or later. (Thistemplate has been designed so that all EndNote generic fields are already typed on **Row 1** of the spreadsheet according to the requirements below.)

8   Place the cursor in **Cell A2** of the Excel worksheet and paste the contents of the clipboard with **[Ctrl]** + **[V]**.

9   You may now modify your data but keep Row 1 with the EndNote field names intact.

10 Save the worksheet as an Excel worksheet, *.xls or *xlsx.

Importing Tab Delimited Data - General

A tab delimited text file that can be imported by EndNote must be structured in one of the following two ways:

a) If same reference types apply to all records then the file may have the following structure:
(^p means line feed and ^t means tab; the field names in the second line are the field names from reference type Generic or from the reference type that will be imported; exact spelling of field names is necessary, all fields must not be present, order between the columns is not critical, empty columns must not exist to the left of the last column.)

```
*Journal Article^p
Author^t    Year^t     Title^t     Journal^t  Volume^t   Etc.^p
<field1>^t <field2>^t <field3>^t <field4>^t <field5>^t Etc.^p
<field1>^t <field2>^t <field3>^t <field4>^t <field5>^t Etc.^p
```

b) If various reference types apply to the records then the file must have the following structure:
(The field names must be those from Reference Type Generic)

```
Reference Type^t    Author^t    Year^t     Title^t     Secondary Title^t Etc.^p
Journal Article ^t <field1>^t <field2>^t <field3>^t <field4>^t         Etc.^p
Book^t             <field1>^t <field2>^t <field3>^t <field4>^t         Etc.^p
```

Any text file that follows the described structures can be imported by EndNote.

♦   **Follow These Steps**

1   Activate the current Library.

2   Go to **File → Import → File...**

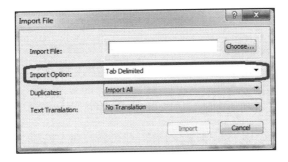

3   Use [**Choose...**] to browse and find the structured text file.

4   Select *Tab Delimited* from the **Import Option** drop-down list.

5   Confirm with [**Import**].

Importing Data from Excel

♦   **Follow These Steps**

1   Open the specially structured Excel worksheet described in previous section.

2   Select all text with [**Ctrl**] + [**A**].

3   Copy the whole document with [**Ctrl**] + [**C**].

4   Create a new document in Microsoft Notes.

5   Paste with [**Ctrl**] + [**V**].

6   Go to **File → Save As...** and determine name file location of the tex tfile.

7   Create a new or open an existing EndNote Library.

8   Go to **File → Import...**

9   Use the [**Choose File...**]-button to browse and find the structured text file.

10   Select *Tab Delimited* from the **Import Option** drop-down list.

11   Confirm with [**Import**].

12   Replace all semicolons plus space in the Library with line feeds using **Edit → Find and Replace** or [**Qtrl**] + [**R**] and type **Find: ;** [**Space**]
and **Replace with:** [**Ctrl**] + [**Enter**] or use [**Insert Special**] and select *Carriage return*.

13   Confirm with [**Change**].

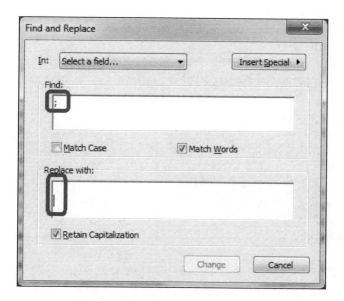

Spell Check

EndNote has a built in Spell checker, which operates on an individual record level.

♦   **Follow These Steps**
1   Activate the current Library.
2   Open the record(s) you wish to spell-check.
3   Go to **Tools → Spell Check**
    or key command **[Ctrl] + [Y]**.

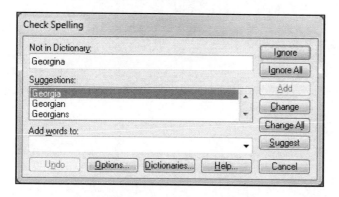

[**Ignore**] means that the word found not to be in the dictionary would be left unchanged

[**Ignore All**] means that all occurrences of the found word will be left unchanged

[**Add**] means that the word found would be added to the current dictionary displayed in the **Add words to**: list box

[**Change**] means that the found word will be replaced by the suggested replacement

[**Change All**] means that all occurrences of the found word will be replaced by the suggested replacement

[**Suggest**] means that a deeper search for replacement is made until the button is disabled

[**Options...**] determines the choice of Main Dictionary language and a number of other options

[**Dictionaries...**] determines what dictionaries are used in addition to the Main Dictionary selected under Options above

The Options and Dictionaries reflect settings made under **Edit →Preferences → Spell Check**, see page 21.

Spelling Options:

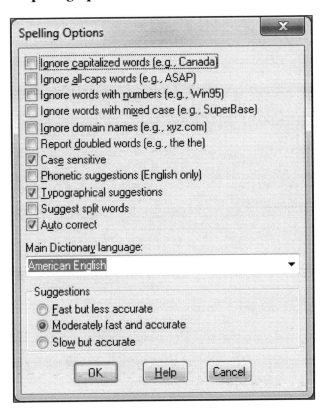

Spelling Dictionaries:

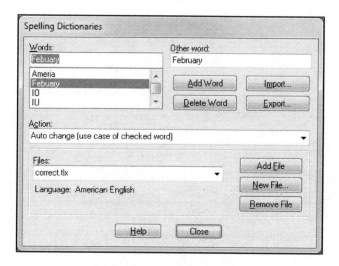

The selected dictionaries are listed in the drop-down list under **Files:**. Existing dictionaries can be added with the [**Add File**]-button or removed with the [**Remove File**]-button.

Under **Words:** are listed such misspelled or other words that should be replaced by words listed under **Other word:**

Here you may add words or terms and its suggested replacement. For each such Word a specific action (6 options) is chosen from the drop-down list. Changes are saved with the [**Add Word**]-button. Words can be deleted with the [**Delete Word**]-button.

Find and Replace Text

Any text in a Library can be changed or deleted in selected records.

♦   **Follow These Steps**
1   Activate the current Library.
2   If all records in the Library will be subject to change(s) apply **References → Show All References** or [**Ctrl**] + [**M**] and proceed to 4 otherwise highlight the records you intend to change.
3   Go to **References → Show Selected References**.
4   Go to **Edit → Find and Replace** or [**Ctrl**] + [**R**].

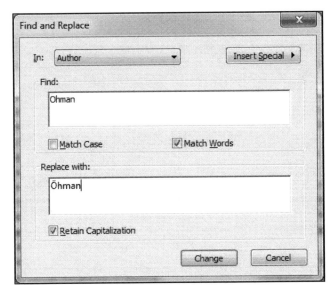

Find and Replace

In: Author ▼   Insert Special ▶

Find:

Ohman

☐ Match Case   ☑ Match Words

Replace with:

Öhman

☑ Retain Capitalization

[Change]   [Cancel]

5   Select a field in the **In:** drop-down list. Type the **Find:** text
    and the **Replace with:** text.
6   Confirm with [**Change**].

Change/Move/Copy Fields

Whole fields can be added, replaced, deleted, or moved in selected
records

♦   **Follow These Steps**
    1   Activate the current Library.
    2   If all records in the Library will be subject to change(s)
        apply **References → Show All References** or [**Ctrl**] + [**M**]
        and proceed to 4 otherwise highlight the records you intend
        to change.
    3   Go to **References → Show Selected References**.
    4   Go to **References → Change/Move/Copy Fields...**

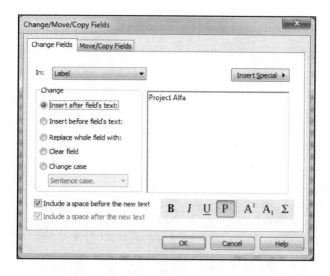

5   The **Change Fields** tab: Select the field that shall be
    modified from the **In:** drop-down list.
6   Select an option under section **Change** and type the text in
    the text box. If you need to type (or start with) line feed
    use **[Ctrl]** + **[Enter]** or **[Insert Special]** and select *Carriage
    return*.
7   Confirm with **[OK]**.

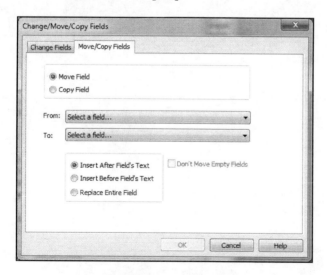

8   The **Move/Copy Fields** tab: Select the From field and the To
    field from the drop-down lists.
9   Select applicable options.
10 Confirm with **[OK]**.

21. MANUSCRIPT TEMPLATES

EndNote includes a large collection of Word Templates that represent a more comprehensive interpretation of author instructions than only how to handle references. These templates incorporate various macros and other help functions for the benefit of scientific writers.

The templates are named after the journals for which they are designed, as they do with the styles. With these templates many formatting issues are already set up for your target publication, such as proper margins, headings, pagination, line spacing, title page, abstract page, graphics placement, and font type, and size. The use of templates can be initiated from either EndNote or Word.

These templates use macros. Occasionally, the macro function in Word can be switched off. Then you need to activate macros and confirm that the source is reliable.

Using Word Templates

◆   **Follow These Steps**
    From EndNote:
    1   Go to **Tools** → **Manuscript Templates**...

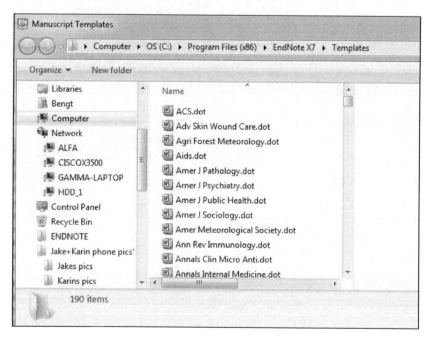

    2   Select a template and confirm with [**Open**].

♦ **Follow These Steps**

From Word:

   1   Create a new document.

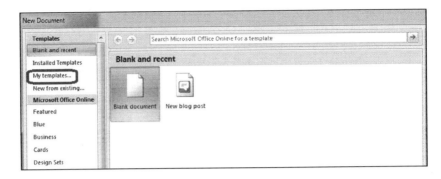

   2   Click **My templates...**

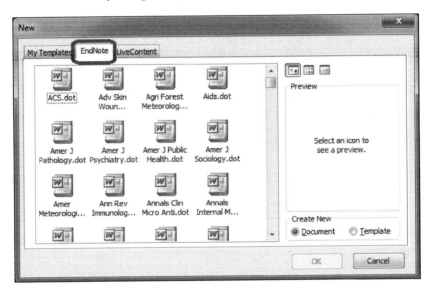

   3   Select the **EndNote** tab.

All templates that are installed with EndNote are ready to be used. If you want to change the view of templates use the buttons in the right hand panel for example view Details:

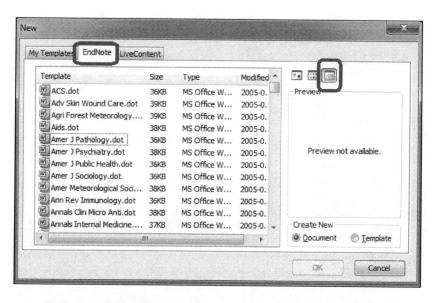

A Wizard will guide you through the most important sections like Title, Author names, Key words etc. We will walk through the template for The Lancet:

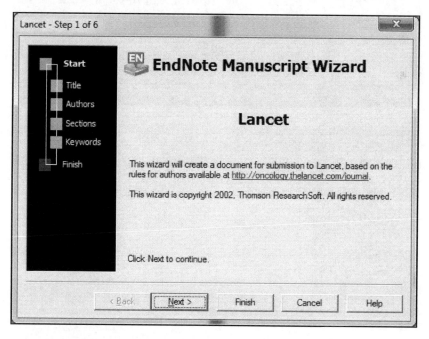

4   Click [**Next >**].

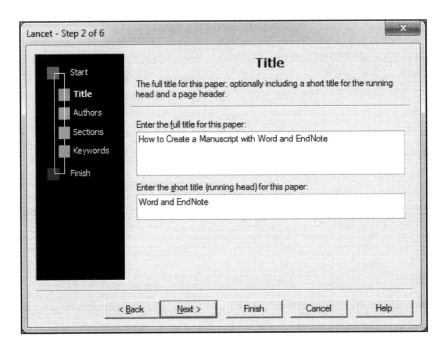

5   Fill in text boxes for the full title and the short title.
     Click [**Next >**].

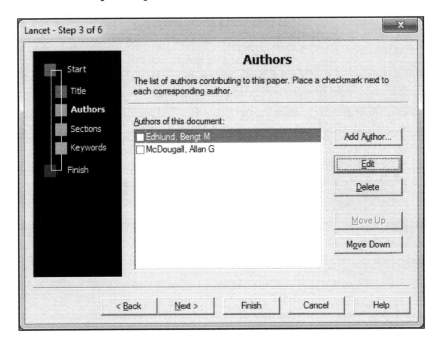

6   Author names and address information can be captured
     from the [**Add Author...**]-button, which also makes it
     possible to connect to Outlook and your address book. Once

authors are listed in your templates they can easily be
added when you create new manuscripts. Click [**Next** >].

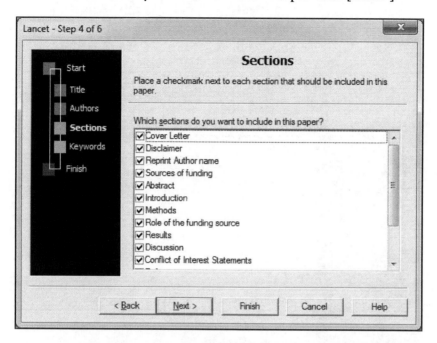

7   You can now select which sections you want to use in your
manuscript. Click [**Nästa** >].

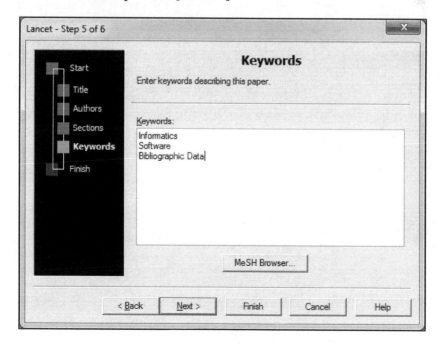

8   The publishers often require a listing of keywords from the
     authors. To facilitate the use of Medical Subheadings, MeSH
     the button [**MeSH-Browser...**] links directly to the
     MeSHbrowser on the Web at National Library of Medicine,
     NLM. The final indexing as applied in PubMed is however in
     the hands of NLM. Click [**Next >**].

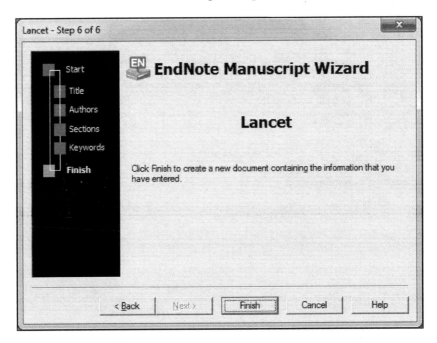

9   Click [**Finish**].

A document created this way also includes all necessary CWYW
settings as dealt with in Chapter 14, page 91. This includes the
selection of Output Style; i.e. the Lancet style has already been
selected. In case you would need some other Style, simply change
before formatting takes place.

All data that we have submitted is now inserted in the Word document. Other data can be filled in on its respective places. Where there is a tag like:

`[Insert Methods here]`

You simply select this tag and overwrite it as you type.

[Insert·Title·of·Article]¶

[Insert·Names·of·Author(s)]¶

[Insert·Affiliation·information·here]¶

[Insert·Disclaimer·here]¶

[Insert·Corresponding·Author·information·here]¶

[Insert·Reprint·Author·name·here]¶

[Insert·Sources·of·funding·here]¶

[Insert·Running·Title·<40·characters]¶

Introduction¶

[Insert·Introduction·text·here]¶

Methods¶

[Insert·Methods·here]¶

Role·of·the·funding·source¶

[Insert·Role·of·the·funding·source·here]¶

Results¶

[Insert·Results]¶

Discussion¶

[Insert·Discussion·here]¶

Conflict·of·Interest·Statements¶

[Insert·Conflict·of·Interest·Statements·here]

References¶

[Insert·Reference·List·here]¶

Tables¶

[Insert·Tables·here·.Each·table·on·its·own·page·]¶

Figures¶

[Insert·Figures·here]¶

Figure·Legends¶

[Insert·Figure·Legends·here]¶

Modifying a Word Template

Word Templates that are delivered as content files included in the EndNote software are created with Microsoft Word. All these templates also incorporate *Macros* and *Wizards*. The templates can be customized in many ways and this instruction will describe how to modify page layout, paragraph styles (fonts, line spacing, indenting etc.), subject headings and alike. Certain structures of the EndNote Template collection must however be kept intact in order to allow the Wizard to work properly.

Most fields can also be changed, but the following fields are required and cannot be deleted:

[Insert Title of Article]

[Insert Names of Author(s)]

[Insert Corresponding Author information here]

[Insert Running Title <40 characters]

[Insert MeSH Keywords 3-10]

[Insert Reference List here]

[Insert Figure Legends here]

The bold black text is compulsory whereas the grey text may be omitted or changed.

Creating a New Template

♦ **Follow These Steps**

1 Start Word.
2 Open an existing Word Template from the EndNote collection using **File → Open...** and navigate to EndNote's template folder, normally C:\Program Files\EndNote\Templates.
3 Go to **File → Save As...** and save the new template with a new name in EndNote's Templates folder with the file extension *.dot or *.dotx.
4 The new template will require an EndNote Style with the same name. Example: A template called *abc.dot* will require an EndNote Style called *abc.ens*.

Modifying the Welcome Screen

You can modify the welcome screen of the Wizard introducing your own text.

♦   **Follow These Steps**

1   Start Word.
2   Open the template.
3   Click the [**Office**]-button.
4   Go to **Prepare → Properties**.
5   Select *Advanced Properties.*
6   In the dialog box <**new template**>**.dot Properties** select the **Summary** tab.
7   Type the name of the journal (or the title you prefer) in the **Title** text box.
8   In the **Comments** text box you can add the title again, add a blank line and then your comments.

Information that has been typed here will be displayed on the welcome page of the Wizard.

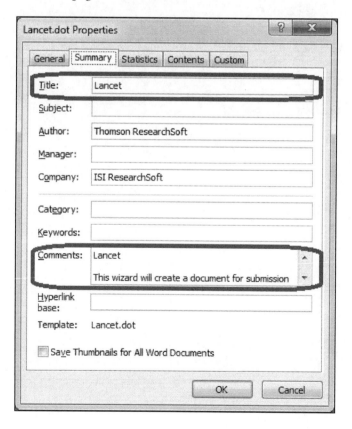

Creating a New Macro Field

When you need a new macro field the easiest way is to copy and paste an existing field and then modify it.

♦ **Follow These Steps**

1   Highlight an existing macro field.

2   Go to **Edit → Copy** or key command **[Ctrl] + [C]**
or right-click and select **Copy**.

3   Move the cursor to the position you want to place the new macro and go to **Edit → Paste**
or **[Ctrl] + [V]**
or right-click and select **Paste**.

4   Position the cursor over the new macro field and right-click and select **Toggle Field Codes**.

5   The text within brackets [..] can now be changed as long as you leave the first word **Insert** intact as being the first word.

6   Highlight the new macro field and right-click and select **Toggle Field Codes**.

7   Go to **File → Save As...** and save the modified template with the same or a new name in EndNote's Templates folder.
Make sure that the document type is Document Template, *.dot or *.dotx.

You have now created a new macro which will become an option in the Wizard under **Sections**.

Adding New Word Paragraph Styles

It is easy to add paragraph styles from existing templates or documents to your customized Word templates.

♦ **Follow These Steps**

   1   Open the Word template that you want to modify.

   2   Go to **Home | Styles | X**
      or **[Alt] + [Ctrl] + [Shift] + [S]**

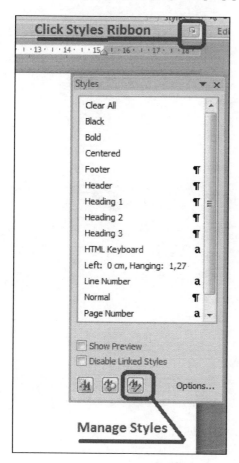

   3   Click **[Manage Styles]**.

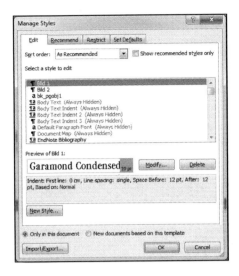

4 Click [**Import/Export...**].

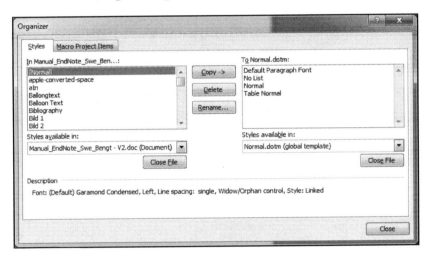

5 The **Styles** tab makes it possible to copy paragraph styles from other associated documents to your current document. You can also close the template Normal.dot with the [**Close File**]-button and when all files are closed then open a new document with [**Open File...**]. From the new document you can copy paragraph styles or other items.

Finally, always test your modified templates. Make sure the templates are saved as a *.dot or *.dotx file and are located in the EndNote template folder. Remember also, that a corresponding Output Style with same file name as the template and with file extension *.ens must be available in EndNote's Styles folder.

Removing Field Codes from Documents Based on Customized Templates

The preferred method of removing field codes from a document based on a Word Template from EndNote's collection is the manual method based on Word's generic command **[Ctrl]** + **[A]**, **[Ctrl]** + **[6]** as described on page 122. Using EndNote's native command **Convert to Plain Text** normally causes linking to the selected template to be replaced by the default template Normal.dot and you may loose most of the paragraph styles and other document settings that you have selected.

22. CITATIONS IN POWERPOINT

EndNote X7 has during its installation also created a new Ribbon called **EndNote X7** in Microsoft PowerPoint:

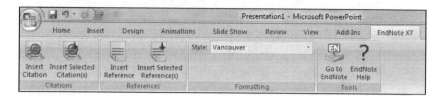

Insert Citation

This option opens the dialog box **EndNote Find & Insert My Citations** and it works according to the description on page 76. EndNote will insert the citations where the cursor is. This function creates only the citation and cannot be formatted and create a bibliography.

Insert Selected Citation(s)

In EndNote select the reference(s) you want to insert. Go to PowerPoint and click this button. EndNote will insert the citations where the cursor is. This function creates only the citation(s) and cannot be formatted and create a bibliography.

Insert Reference

This option opens the dialog box **EndNote Find & Insert My References** and it works according to the description on page 76. EndNote will insert the bibliography where the cursor is. After the insertion the bibliography is created based on the current Style.

Insert Selected Reference(s)

In EndNote select the reference(s) you want to insert. Go to PowerPoint and click this button. EndNote will insert the bibliography where the cursor is. After the insertion the bibliography is created based on the current Style.

Output Styles Menu

This option is used when you want to find a certain Style. You need to select Style before you insert citations and bibliographies in PowerPoint as it is not possible to re-format a citation or bibliography with an alternative Style after an insertion has been made.

Go to EndNote Command

If EndNote is running this button will switch you over to EndNote. If EndNote is not running then it will start.

- ♦ -

The function *Insert Selected Reference(s)* can also be made with the *Copy Formatted* command, [**Ctrl**] + [**K**], as was discussed on page 93.

First select Style and then select and highlight records in the EndNote Library, apply [**Ctrl**] + [**K**], switch over to PowerPoint, decide the insertion position and finally paste with [**Ctrl**] + [**V**].

23. ENDNOTE ONLINE

This Chapter is in detail valid for EndNote X7 and may to partly be applicable for earlier versions of EndNote.

EndNote Online, earlier EndNote Web, is a service initially created for beginners and students on the following conditions:

The user shall belong to an organization who subscribes that subscribes on Thomson's databases Web-of-Science or Web-of-Knowledge.

From EndNote X2.0.1 (a "patched" EndNote X2) all licensees have the right to create and use an EndNote Online account.

Users without a valid EndNote license who still have the right to create and use an EndNote Web account can instead use an EndNote Online plug-in (free).

The service allows storing references on Thomson's web and also using the CWYW-features with EndNote Online plug-in and a compatible word processor.

The average EndNote user can benefit from EndNote Online by storing selected references on a web and make them accessible for a work group. The total number of references for each account is limited to 50,000 and can be divided into several groups.

Creating an EndNote Online Account

You can create an EndNote Online account by going to `http://www.myendnoteweb.com`:

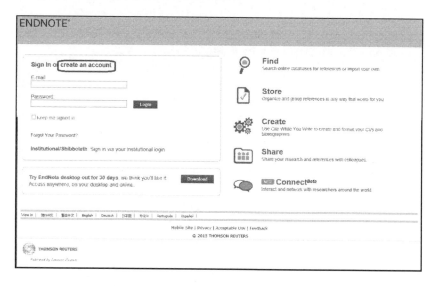

You are transferred to a form where you fill in some personal data and create the account. When you hold the account you can use this page to log in and check *Keep me logged in.*

Syncing is the Normal Mode

♦ **Follow These Steps**

1 Open the Library you intend to use for syncing.

2 Go to **Edit → Preferences** and the section **Sync**.

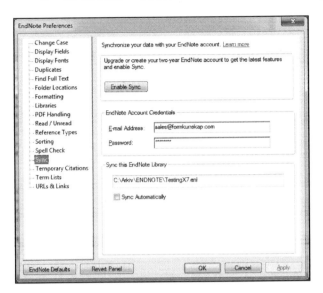

3 Fill in your account details.

4 Choose *Sync Automatically* (every 15th minute) and click
[**Enable Sync**]. You might also need to log in to your
EndNote Online account.

5 Click [**OK**].

It may take some time (minutes) when you sync for the first time.
You can also sync manually by going to **Tools → Sync**

or the icon

The text box with the name of the Library for syncing is write
protected as EndNote selects the current Library for syncing. It
means that when you create or open a new Library and initiate sync
with **Tools → Sync** EndNote asks if you intend to change Library. If
you accept your Online Library and your current Library will merge
when syncing has been completed. You can however refrain from
syncing.

Whenever you need you can reach EndNote Online with **Help →
EndNote Online**.

Your EndNote Online Library may look like this:

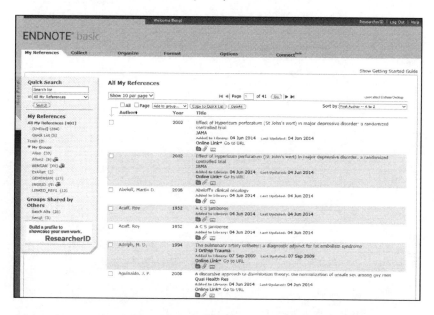

Syncing means that both Libraries are kept identical concerning
records, groups (not smart groups), attachments, and figures and
tables. Any change can be made either in the Online Library or in
your (desktop) EndNote Library and the update or syncing is always
made in both directions. Syncing can however only be initiated from
EndNote desktop.

Manual Transfer of References

It is possible to manually transfer references between the platforms.
This is made by exporting from either platform using an export
format for example RIS-format, and then import to the other
platform using the corresponding filter.

CWYW with EndNote Online

This section is valid for users of EndNote X, X1 – X7 and holders of
EndNote Online plugin.

From Word:

♦ **Follow These Steps**

   1   Go to **EndNote | Tools | Preferences**
       or key command [**Alt**] + [**9**].

   2   Choose the **Application** tab.

3 Choose *EndNote online* on the **Application**: drop-down list, fill in the other details and click [**OK**].

When you have logged in on EndNote Online the EndNote ribbon in Word has changed and looks like this:

This ribbon is exactly the same as when you only use EndNote Online plugin.

The functions are the same as in EndNote, but Go to EndNote Online brings us to EndNote Online (you may have to log in again) and the Library looks like this:

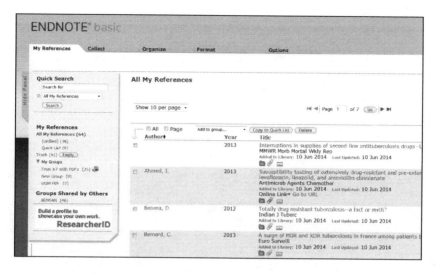

The tabs have the following functions:

My References: Handles your Library and your groups.

Collect: Here you can go online to free databases or log in with your account. Here are also import functions of structured text files.

Organize: Here you can manage your groups and decide which groups you will share with other users.

Format: Here you select your favorite Styles and can mail bibliographies using selected Style formats. Here are also export functions of structured text files.

Options: Here you can change password to your EndNote Online account.

Syncing of Shared Groups

When you create shared groups for members of your team a few functions and options are important. A Library is synced and controlled only by *one* person. *Shared groups should therefore be read only* otherwise the colleagues can change, add or delete records. Shared groups can not accommodate attachments thus not any PDF documents.

When your teammate shall work with records from a shared Library the records must be transferred to any desktop Library. The procedure is often copying shared groups and pasting to his/her EndNote Online Library and then syncing with an EndNote desktop Library or export (RIS-format) and then import to the EndNote desktop Library.

24. SHARING LIBRARIES

EndNote X7.2 introduced improved file sharing of Libraries for closed user groups. The conditions for such sharing is that all members of the group must have EndNote X7.2 and a valid EndNote Online account. There must be a dedicated administrator maintaining a working synced Library. The administrator can invite up to 14 other users.

♦   **Follow These Steps**
    1   Go to **File → Share...**

       or the icon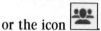

The invitee will now get a mail which must be acknowledged with his/her EndNote Online account.

When this is all done then the invitee has access to the shared Library:

♦   **Follow These Steps**
    1   Go to **File → Open Shared Library...**
       or key command **[Ctrl] + [Shift] + [O]**.

Access is now offered to all shared Libraries as invitations from other groups could have been made earlier.

- ♦ -

The administrator must have a synced Library which now will be shared including all its auxiliary items. The Library has no size limitation. All functionalities are kept intact in a shared Library including attached files (PDF:s, graphic files and tables), PDF notations, Custom Groups and Smart Groups.

Shared Libraries cannot be write protected meaning that any group member can modify records, add or delete records or add or delete attachments. All such modifications will be immediately available to the whole group. Group members can use a shared Library for any type of work, but only the administrator can sync to his/her own Library.

- ♦ -

Important to distinguish between a *Shared Group* and a *Shared Library.*

The Shared Group is dealt with in Chapter 23, page 155. A Shared Group is in a better control by the administrator as he/she can decide about read/write properties. The person who shares this group must copy records from the shared group to his/her own Online Library before such records can be used in his/her own synced Library. Attached files (PDF and other) can cannot be included in shared groups.

25. STORING IN DROPBOX AND OTHER CLOUD SERVICES

Dropbox is an established cloud service for file sharing in closed user groups. Dropbox can be used for sharing EndNote Libraries bibliotek with the following remarks.

Use compressed EndNote Libraries for such storing with the file extension *.enlx as then the whole structure is complete with folders and attachments.

♦ **Follow These Steps**

1   Open the Library.
2   Go to **File → Compressed Library (enlx)...**

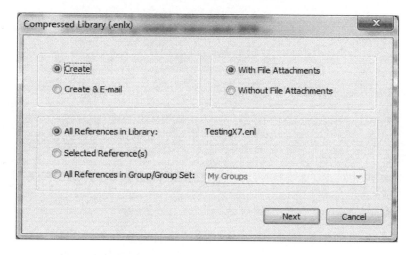

3   Select *Create*.
4   Select *With File Attachments* and *All References in Library*.
5   Click [**Next**].
6   Decide location and file name for example your Dropbox folder.
7   Click [**Save**].

The compressed file shall now be shared by the team members. It is considered risky to open and work directly in a file stored in Dropbox. That goes for many applications and file formats and also for EndNote Libraries. The person who has access to a shared EndNote Library should therefore download to a desktop computer and open and decompress from there. The unpacked Library is identical with the original in all respects: record numbers, attachments, PDF:s, custom groups, smart groups and term lists. Updating of a shared Library is a bit tricky as each time the Library is uncompressed the whole Library is created again and with the same name. An alternative structure could be that you build sections of references in smaller Libraries that you can merge when uncompressed.

163

26. SUPPORT, TRAINING AND VARIOUS HELPERS

As a holder of this book you are welcome to contact **support@formkunskap.com** or Skype **bengt.edhlund** in any matter that has to do with installation problems or user procedures as described in this book. If you or your institution need training, special courses or consultations you can also contact **info@formkunskap.com**. We have trained around 1,000 EndNote-users throughout the years, mostly in Sweden, Norway and Canada.

We summarize the other functions that keep track of the current status of your EndNote installation, your Libraries and other useful resources.

Status Records

Tools → Library Summary...
References → Record Summary...
Help → About EndNote X7...

Support Resources

Help → Search for Help on... or **[F1]**
Help → Getting Started with EndNote
Help → Online User Guide
Help → Get Technical Support
Help → EndNote Tutorials and More
Help → Search Knowledgebase

Other Helpers

Help → EndNote Output Style (connects to EndNote's Style Finder)
Help → Check for Updates...
Help → Welcome to EndNote (Online account and Syncing)
Help → EndNote Online (takes you to EndNote Online Library)
Help → Activate EndNote
Help → Download EndNote Plugin (various plugins)

Discussion forums

Help → EndNote Community (a forum for discussions)

APPENDIX A – KEY COMMANDS

Listed below are some of the most useful key commands. Many of these strictly adhere to general Windows conventions. Some are specific for each program.

Windows	Word	EndNote	Key Commandso	Descriptions
✓	✓	✓	[Ctrl] + [C]	Copy
		✓	[Ctrl] + [K]	Copy Formatted
✓	✓	✓	[Ctrl] + [X]	Cut
✓	✓	✓	[Ctrl] + [V]	Paste
✓	✓	✓	[Ctrl] + [A]	Select/Unselect All
✓	✓	✓	[Ctrl] + [O]	Open Document/Library
		✓	[Ctrl]+[Shift]+[O]	Open Shared Library
		✓	[Ctrl] + [F]	Search References
		✓	[Ctrl] + [PgUp]	Previous Reference
		✓	[Ctrl] + [PgDn]	Next Reference
	✓		[Ctrl] + [G]	Go To
		✓	[Ctrl] + [G]	Open Link
✓	✓	✓	[Ctrl] + [N]	New Document/Reference
		✓	[Ctrl] + [E]	Edit References
		✓	[Ctrl] + [D]	Delete References
✓	✓	✓	[Ctrl] + [P]	Print Document/References
		✓	[Ctrl] + [R]	Find and Replace
✓	✓	✓	[Ctrl] + [S]	Save
		✓	[Ctrl] + [Q]	Exit Program
		✓	[Ctrl] + [1]	Open List
		✓	[Ctrl] + [3]	Link Term Lists
		✓	[Ctrl] + [4]	Define Term Lists
✓	✓	✓	[Ctrl] + [W]	Close Window
✓	✓	✓	[Ctrl]+[Shift]+[W]	Close all Windows of same Type
		✓	[Ctrl] + [Y]	Spell Check

Windows	Word	EndNote	Key Commands	Description
	✓	✓	[Ctrl] + [Z]	Undo
	✓		[Ctrl] + [B]	Find
	✓		[Ctrl] + [H]	Replace
	✓	✓	[Alt] + [1]	Toggle between EndNote/Word
	✓	✓	[Alt] + [2]	Insert Citation(s)
	✓	✓	[Alt] + [3]	Format Bibliography
	✓		[Alt] + [4]	Unformat Citation(s)
	✓		[Alt] + [5]	Show/Edit Library Reference(s)
	✓		[Alt] + [6]	Edit Citation(s)
	✓		[Alt] + [7]	Find Citation(s)
	✓	✓	[Alt] + [8]	Import/Export Traveling Library
	✓	✓	[Alt] + [9]	CWYW Preferences
	✓		[Alt] + [0]	Insert Note
	✓		[Ctrl] + [6]	Unlink Fields
	✓		[Ctrl]+[Alt]+[F]	Insert Footnote
		✓	[Ctrl]+[Alt]+[P]	Open Attachment

APPENDIX B – THREE STEPS TO CAPTURE REFERENCES

Step 1: You receive an alert email from your Saved Searches with *What's New* periodically. Click on the **View** link and you log in directly to your **My NCBI** account and display the all new records:

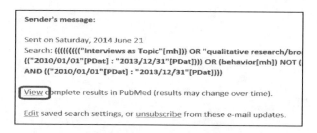

Step 2: In PubMed you decide what records you want to capture. No selection means all displayed records. Go to **Send to**, select *Citation manager* and click on [**Create File**]:

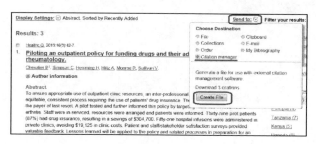

Step 3: Your default reference handling software (for example EndNote) starts and an import mode is activated automatically and the records are transferred with a preselected filter:

Record	Author	Year	Title	Rating	Journal	Ref Type	URL
710	Burge, F.; Lawso...	2013	Assessing the feasibility of extracting clinical in...		Healthc Q	Journal Article	
709	Chevalier, B.; Si...	2013	Piloting an outpatient policy for funding drugs ...		Healthc Q	Journal Article	
711	Tait, G. R.; Hodg...	2013	Residents learning from a narrative experienc...		Adv Health Sci ...	Journal Article	http://link.s

Now your new records are ready to be used depending on your research situation and need. Often you need to capture the full text material (PDF). Eventually you will need to upgrade your references from PubMed when the Medline indexing has been completed as Premedline and Publisher supported records are normally short of Abstract and MeSH terms. You may also export reference data including full-text articles to any analytic qualitative software (for example NVivo) for further text and content analysis, which is typically the case for literature reviews. Especially powerful is the Framework method as established by National Center for Social Research (NatCen) in U.K.

INDEX

31147508R00097

Made in the USA
Middletown, DE
20 April 2016